BUYING PROF
(sec

BUYING PROPERTY IN PORTUGAL

(second edition)

GABRIELLE COLLISON

First Published in Great Britain 2007
by Book Shaker

Second Edition Published in Great Britain 2011
by Summertime Publishing

Edited by Sam Parfitt

For all those people who forced
me out of my comfort zones.

Praise for This Book

Gabrielle once again hits the mark. Don't even think about moving to Portugal without it!

Simon Pownall
Owner of www.expatsportugal.com

Moving home is stressful. Throw in a foreign country, an unfamiliar language, different laws and customs and even the most desirable property can become the stuff of nightmares. So when I started my searches in Portugal it was a blessed relief to find a book that simply 'told it like it is'. With simple checklists supported by more detailed explanations, the pros and cons of various options laid out in an easy-to-read manner and neither over-hyped nor forbidding. There is no one route to find the perfect 'place-in-the-sun' but this book will be a wise and trusty companion along your way.

Tim Serle

Having travelled to the Algarve region of Portugal on numerous occasions, my wife and I are considering options for buying a home there. This book is an invaluable resource for anyone looking to purchase in Portugal. Particularly useful are the sections covering the pros and cons of the various buying options and different types of location. Having specific information on the Algarve also meant help is provided for our particular area of interest. A must read for all would be Portuguese settlers!

Nick Bussey

Regulations and laws change at a bewildering speed in Portugal and so an up to date book is essential. This one goes much further than others by explaining every step and the potential pitfalls. As well as suggesting that you check the qualifications of a stated professional and the status of a property, it tells you the department that holds that information, the relevant website to visit and then — and this is its genius — it guides the non-Portuguese reader on how to correctly use the site and gather information. You will be amazed at the volume of information you can extract once armed with this powerful book and careful reading will hopefully prevent many expensive mistakes being made.

I recommend it not only for its meticulous detail and practical advice, but because the writer obviously knows the people, the property world and the country very well indeed. It is written in an honest, unsentimental style and when I'd finished I felt I understood the nature of the place a little more.

Kim Thomas

Another clear, concise and compact guide to buying property in Portugal by Gabrielle Collison. This 2nd edition is jam packed with invaluable information for potential buyers and investors. At times, Portuguese bureaucracy can be extremely daunting, especially if you are not familiar with the language. Gabrielle's book is easy to follow and will set your mind at ease, allowing you the confidence to follow your dreams with your eyes open! Even if you have purchased the first edition and feel that you are well equipped with the knowledge to buy in Portugal I'd highly recommend that you get the 2nd edition, simply because changes occur on a regular basis in Portugal and what may have been relevant in 2007 will almost certainly not be in 2011.

Karen Connolly

Acknowledgements

I'd like to thank all those who contributed short stories about their move to Portugal, and especially to Nicky Carter of *www.gekkoportugal.com* for her added help and input.

Contents

Introduction

If you're thinking of buying a property in Portugal and want to get things right first time – then this straightforward little guide has been written for you.

But why should you take my advice and how does this book differ from all the other stuff you could read? Well to find out, read on…

My family bought a property in the Algarve in 2000, which inevitably meant that I began spending more and more time in Portugal.

Due to the fact that I love learning languages and had already learnt Spanish, French and some Italian, I picked up a working knowledge of Portuguese fairly quickly.

On hearing that I was conversant in the language, many non-Portuguese-speaking friends and acquaintances started asking me to do them small favours.

While doing these favours, I visited more than my fair share of local government departments, authorities, utility companies and businesses to sort out various problems, in particular those surrounding property purchases.

I soon began to realise that a fair number of the people I was helping had been caught out by their lack of knowledge of the bureaucracy, and their unfamiliarity with the language. Several of them had also been far too trusting and naïve.

The property world is naturally a cutthroat one and while many purchases go through smoothly, there are others that could only be described as 'nightmares'!

Little by little, I learnt all about property documents and the processes involved in buying a property in Portugal, and I started to write about the potential pitfalls on various Internet forums.

My reputation for being fairly knowledgeable soon spread and other people started to contact me for help and advice. I was also invited to appear on Kiss FM's *Straight Talk with Phill Gilbert*, a phone-in radio show in the Algarve, and later asked to assist with the filming of a TV programme about relocating to Portugal.

Writing a book therefore seemed the logical next step and provides me with a way to help even more people navigate the Portuguese property market.

This is the second edition and I hope it is even more comprehensive than the first.

Now, I will warn you — this book is not your typical 'buying abroad' book. It isn't written to encourage you to buy a place in Portugal. If you're already keen on Portugal then you don't need me to persuade you —

you just need to know what you have to do next and how to get things right.

There are many other books out there giving general property information and travel advice on Portugal but my aim is to give specific, and hopefully more streetwise, advice that might just save you a lot of time and a little money in the process.

This book will help you get your thinking cap on about buying a property in Portugal and the things you should check for yourself, whether you decide to use legal representation or not.

While I'm on the subject of legal representation, let me just make something clear – this book is not in any way advising you to shun legal advice and 'go it alone' when buying property in Portugal. Unfortunately, mistakes can still be made despite doing exhaustive checks and searches. However, by using reputable, independent legal advice, alongside doing your own thorough checks, this will no doubt lessen your chances of running into problems.

It should also be noted that changes in this area are frequent, and while I have endeavoured to make this book as accurate and as up-to-date as possible, some websites may still have changed since publication.

Likewise, different areas and regions in Portugal often interpret the laws and regulations in their own unique way and this can sometimes lead to confusion when making general statements for the country as a whole.

The best advice in relation to buying a property in Portugal, or in any country in the world come to that, is that while respecting the local business culture, only do as you would be happy to do back home.

Do not worry about appearing difficult or demanding and do not feel embarrassed to keep asking as many questions as you wish. Buying a property is obviously a very expensive and potentially risky business.

If you do not take precautions and fail to investigate thoroughly, you could end up paying dearly further down the line.

I hope this book serves as a practical and reliable resource when buying property in Portugal and I wish you *boa sorte* (good luck)!

Gabrielle Collison
www.gabriellecollison.com

Don’t Be So Trusting

Up until recently, 1974 in fact, Portugal was under a tightly controlled, fascist regime.

During the fascist era there was an atmosphere of fear. People kept things very much to themselves and families stuck closely together.

The government was seen as the enemy and the average person was frightened of officialdom.

Nepotism and cronyism were normal and sometimes, whole families controlled municipal councils and certain jobs. Corruption was rife with a heavy controlling bureaucracy.

Although Portugal has made great strides forward in recent years with the Internet having a huge impact on record keeping and reducing bureaucracy, old attitudes and ideas still linger and seem to be only very slowly dying out.

The above factors, together with rampant tax evasion, according to a recent World Bank report, are still holding Portugal back from competing with the rest of Europe.

It also seems to be the opinion of many Portuguese people I have met and chatted to over the course of my time in Portugal.

On the face of it, the Portuguese seem very welcoming, friendly and accommodating to foreigners and this is true to a large extent. They can also be very helpful, going out of their way to assist at times.

However, people are people and one must also bear in mind that many areas in Portugal, for example the Algarve, only survive due to tourism and property development. Therefore, a smiling, welcoming face may not always be genuine.

Both Portuguese and fellow nationals, who profess to be your good friend, may later on show themselves to be anything but and seemingly charming people may turn out to be nothing more than polished actors.

The lure of the Euro sign can be just too much for some people and if there is a chance to make money at your expense then it might well happen. This is a sad fact of life in any country, and Portugal is no exception, so don't let your guard down for one minute!

Never let anyone else, including 'professionals', take control of your life and your finances without first checking them out thoroughly and obtaining independent references. While very rare, there have been cases of 'professionals' absconding with people's money, so it is always best to 'err on the side of caution' when dealing with people.

Both Portuguese and expatriates will sometimes speak of doing things the 'old Portuguese way'. This usually refers to a more laid-back and casual method of buying property without using any legal advice (and trying to avoid paying as much tax as possible). It used to be the way for many years in Portugal.

However, I would not recommend this as an approach to buying property, especially for foreigners. If something was to go wrong, you could find yourself having all sorts of problems in the future. Please, be careful!

Relocating

People on holiday can often be seen staring dreamily into real estate agents' windows.

When you're in a holiday mood with the sun shining and wine flowing, Portugal can seem like paradise. However, the worst thing you could possibly do during this holiday state of mind is to suddenly decide that Portugal is the place you want to live and start viewing properties and put a deposit down for one.

As with all big decisions in life, research is the key and one must always remember that *living* somewhere is completely different to *holidaying* there.

Even if you are just thinking in terms of a holiday home, a lot of careful consideration needs to be given, especially if you are going to need rental income to sustain your venture. More and more people have bought holiday homes over the last few years, so competition can be fierce to get your property rented out.

You should do some thorough research on the likely income you will receive *after* you have paid for taxes, cleaning and laundry, condominium charges (if on a complex) and regular maintenance to the property.

Upkeeping a property to a decent standard can work out a lot more expensive than you might think!

Another thing to consider when buying a holiday home is the best location for holiday rentals and what type of clientele you want to attract. If you would like to have a remote, countryside location but the more popular rentals are on the livelier coast, then you may have to compromise a little.

Obviously the summer months will be the peak time for rentals and income and therefore you might only get to use your property during the colder, rainier months. Is this something that suits you or are you prepared to forgo some of your income?

If you are looking for an investment then you need to speak to independent, overseas financial consultants to see what the long-term and short-term capital growth opportunities are likely to be. What might suit one investor might not suit another, so it is imperative that you seek sound, qualified advice.

Relocating on a permanent basis to another country, especially one which has a different language and culture, needs thorough planning. If you have children and need to work, this is even more crucial. Finding work in Portugal, if you do not speak fluent Portuguese, is not at all easy and even then you will find that many jobs only pay the minimum wage. In 2010 this was €475 a month, expecting to rise to €500 in 2011.

Now, for those of you thinking that you will only be working amongst the expatriate community and that you will find plenty of work, with little need to learn Portuguese, please think again! Foreigners have been coming to live in Portugal, particularly the Algarve, for many years and a lot of potential business opportunities have become over-saturated.

You must also consider the fact that many Portuguese (and the increasing Eastern European population in Portugal) speak excellent English and can offer the same services a lot cheaper.

Having enough money behind you to live for a minimum of one year without having to work, is a wise move and certainly important if you are trying out a business venture to see if it might work. You will really need some form of security behind you.

Those with businesses, which can be run from anywhere in the world via the Internet, or retirees with generous pensions, and/or alternative income and savings, generally survive the best in Portugal.

If you have children, what about schooling? Will you be sending your children to the local school or to a private, fee-paying, international school? If so, can you afford this? What age are your children and are they at a stage in their life where they will pick up the language and integrate easily? It is generally considered that before the age of seven is best.

So think carefully. You don't want to put your family through the misery and upheaval of relocating only to have to return through lack of research and doing something on a whim.

Ask yourself why you really want to relocate and what you hope to gain from it. Many people cite reasons, such as:

- ❑ Less crime.
- ❑ Better life for their children.
- ❑ Warmer climate.
- ❑ Less stress.
- ❑ Lower cost of living.
- ❑ Better standard of living.

However, do your research to see if those things are actually true in the area you are hoping to live. Often the reality is quite different from the perception.

While some of Portugal is lost in a timewarp, and still rather old-fashioned, quiet and quaint, other parts (particularly the major cities) are like anywhere else in modern 21st Century Europe.

Also, if you are someone who gets impatient when waiting for more than two minutes in the post office to be served, then think long and hard about living in Portugal or you could end up more stressed out than ever! The Portuguese generally do things in their own good time and won't be hurried by you tapping your fingers on the counter, or tutting loudly.

In addition, Portuguese bureaucracy can have you wandering around in complete circles for hours, if not days and months on end. Read Portuguese newspapers and websites, and expatriate magazines and forums to get a feel for the country and its problems, as well as its obvious advantages.

Renting for an extended period of time is an excellent idea. This will give you the opportunity to look around the area you are thinking of relocating to as a native in order to make sure it is what you really want. It will also give you the opportunity to check out other areas around Portugal.

You could also consider renting out your home in the UK or other country of origin to see if Portugal is for you before selling up lock, stock and barrel. This way you will always have something to return to should the need arise.

Experiencing all the seasons is a must too. Hot, sunny Portugal can also be cold, wet and windy at times and remember that most houses do not have central heating and often get very damp.

Other things that you may wish to consider are:

- ❑ Is a coastal area, while nice in the winter, going to be too busy and noisy in the summer?
- ❑ Is a place that is lively and entertaining in the summer going to be too dead and dull in the winter?

- ❑ What are the local amenities and services on offer? What is the local transport like?
- ❑ Do you need a lot of social contact, or are you happy to live quite remote and isolated?
- ❑ Do you want or need the support of fellow nationals around you, or do you want to be a million miles away from the nearest expat?

Make a list of the things you really need and want and those you definitely don't. Being far away from the nearest shops and banks can seem bearable during a two week holiday, but on a daily basis it may become extremely irritating.

Whatever you do, don't hurry into a decision. Take your time. There are plenty of properties for sale out there, so don't get caught in the 'scarcity' trap that vendors use to improve their profits.

Also try not to set yourself impossible schedules and deadlines to view and buy a property. A few days or a long weekend is rarely enough time to consider things properly or to do the necessary checks.

If you are retiring to Portugal, then you should still do some thorough research. If you are fit and able living somewhere remote might not be a problem. However, if you have any medical issues then living somewhere closer to health centres and other amenities might be a wiser option.

Another factor to consider might be how you wish to spend your retirement. For some, a quiet life of gardening and reading in a countryside location is ideal. For others, a more active social life might be desirable. Check what is on offer to you in the areas you are looking at and whether this suits you.

It goes without saying that sound financial planning for your retirement is a must. The cost of living in Portugal, especially in certain areas, is no longer as cheap as it used to be and one should always take inflation into account. The fluctuation in the value of Sterling to the Euro has also meant that many retirees have struggled over the last year or so to make ends meet, and some have even had to sell up and return home.

Speak to an expert financial consultant, who is knowledgeable about both Portugal and your country of origin, in terms of making the most out of your pension or other savings and investments. You should also consider discussing your tax liabilities, and estate planning and inheritance.

CASE STUDY: DEREK HARPER & NICKY CARTER

Derek and I first visited Portugal in 2003, when we toured all over the country from Aveiro in the north, down the Silver Coast, inland to Castelo Branco and through the Alentejo to the Algarve. However, the region we felt most at home in was Central Portugal†. The rolling hills, rivers and lakes mixed with the wealth of historic towns and villages ensured there was enough for us to enjoy while being able to relax in a semi-rural setting.

We didn't settle in Portugal until 2004. After spending six months living in the Algarve, we purchased a stone farmhouse ruin close to Castelo do Bode Lake at Martinchel††. The property was in a derelict state and required complete reconstruction, but the location was ideal. Ten minutes walk into the village, a further five to the lake's edge and only a ten-minute drive into the town of Abrantes — and three major towns within easy reach.

We had intended to spend our early retirement restoring the property to its former glory, but while we waited for the planning approvals to be granted by the town hall, we were inundated with requests from family and friends wanting to come out to Portugal to visit an area that, up until that point, they had never heard of. While here, the majority decided to purchase property as holiday homes as they too fell in love with the area.

We helped them find estate agents, properties and lawyers, and helped with connections to public utilities. In fact, most of our time was spent emailing back and forth about the different activities, restaurants and so on in the area. When *their* friends and families started emailing us as well, Derek and I decided to build an information website, as we thought this would be easier for everyone, ourselves included! However, when *www.gekkoportugal.com* launched, it had the reverse effect and we have been inundated with emails and requests for information on living, working and buying property in Portugal ever since.

We advertised a selection of properties for sale in the area with the local agents' permission, but many who emailed found it difficult dealing with local agents, who lacked the urgency to respond with relevant or correct information. After some discussions with our friend Claudia Silva, who had been in the real estate industry in Portugal for over 10 years, we decided to form our own estate agency, Chavetejo, to ensure we could look after customers according to our own high standards. Based in the historic town of Tomar[†††], our agency covers a huge region encompassing the Silver Coast, parts of the Alentejo, Beiras and Ribatejo.

Forming the company was relatively simple; indeed the actual formation took less than a day. However, we couldn't officially open the doors to our offices for another three months, until we had received an estate agency licence. Unfortunately, the bureaucracy in Portugal can be a bit of a nightmare and things do tend to take longer to get approved, stamped and signed.

Running a business in Portugal is fairly straightforward. As the country is part of the EU, many of the rules and regulations are similar to those in the UK. Both Derek and I ran our own businesses in the UK at various times and there are only a few differences that we have come across. Here in Portugal, an accountant doesn't just do your tax returns – they're a source of great knowledge and worth every penny. Not speaking the language is probably the biggest hurdle to setting up and running a business here.

It's been over three years since we opened our agency and we have helped hundreds of people from all over the world find their dream homes in the sun and provided thousands more with information on the country and particular procedures.

I can't think of any regrets, but mistakes we've made aplenty! When moving to any foreign country, where the language and culture are new, you will make mistakes. Whether in conversation or social etiquette, it's inevitable that you will get things wrong. The key is to take it all in your stride and not take it too seriously.

For example, Derek went to the local builders merchant to buy 15 metres of grey drainage tubing and couldn't understand why everyone was laughing at him. He eventually got some help from a friendly customer, who explained that he had been asking for a 15-metre ashtray. Derek did eventually get the pipe.

Although living in Portugal has many pros, there are downsides too, which are often not that well publicised. Unfortunately, Portuguese companies and official government bodies do like their paperwork, usually in triplicate, and I am afraid there is a tendency to pass the buck, which can leave you going round in circles at times.

†The central region is made up of parts of Montanhas, the Silver Coast and the Alentejo/Ribatejo.

††Castelo do Bode Lake is Portugal's second largest reservoir and is a haven for birds and wildlife. It even has its own eco-museum based in the village of Martinchel. The dam is an impressive structure and is a popular tourist spot for the Portuguese. During most weekends and holidays, there are stalls selling dried fruits and traditional crafts.

†††Tomar (Ribatejo) is a town steeped in history and home to the UNESCO-listed *Convento do Cristo*. The town straddles the Nabão river and has two distinct areas – the old town, with cobbled streets and ancient buildings and squares, and the new town, with avenues of shops, apartment blocks and supermarkets.

Nicky Carter & Derek Harper,
Tomar, Central Portugal
www.gekkoportugal.com
www.chavetejo.com

Learning Portuguese

Learning Portuguese is crucial, unless you want to live in an 'expat bubble' and not integrate, or have no wish to understand anything about the society in which you are living.

To rely on other people to do things for you is also very annoying and frustrating, and in the unfortunate event of an emergency occurring, it could be dangerous or even life threatening if you can't speak Portuguese. Learning the language can also help prevent you from being taken advantage of.

You should not only consider the benefits to you, but the fact that many Portuguese natives will find it extremely impolite and somewhat arrogant, if you are making no effort to speak to them in their language.

While tourist areas and more cosmopolitan towns and cities may have many English speakers to hand, small towns and villages will not. Government offices and authorities will rarely deal with you in English, and if you attempt to write communications in English you may well get a terse reply telling you that the working language of Portugal is Portuguese!

I have heard many an expat excuse, for example: the Portuguese like to practise their English, the world language is now English, they always reply back to me in English when I try to speak Portuguese, it is a difficult language, we don't have time as we've been so busy since arriving. The list is endless.

It is no good waiting until you are living in Portugal to learn and hoping you will just pick it up. You won't! You should start learning many months before your permanent arrival and keep doing it after your relocation. You cannot avoid studying if you really want to learn a new skill.

If you are not going to learn the language, or really feel you can't (although quite often people convince themselves they can't do things when it isn't actually the case) then you must seriously consider whether you should be moving in the first place.

OK, I have been hard on you – so what are my tips for making it easier to learn Portuguese?

- There are many language books, tapes, CDs and courses out there. Some are better than others and some may suit people better than others. Buying a few different courses and alternating them, while expensive, may help to keep things fresh and widen your vocabulary and grammar.
- The key is little and often. Studying 15 to 20 minutes a day is far better than an hour or two once or twice a week. You will retain a lot more and not find yourself getting bogged down with it and bored. You are also more likely to make

that amount of time available each day and not find excuses for doing something else.

- If possible, try to find a private, native speaking teacher and either attend a class, or preferably one-to-one lessons, so that you can study at your own pace.
- Study with a spouse, partner or friend for motivational purposes. If you both know there is a time set and that someone else is relying on you, you will be less likely to skip it and do something else.
- Try to find a non-English-speaking friend or friends.
- Watch Portuguese TV and listen to Portuguese radio. However awful some of the programmes might be, you will be amazed at how much sinks in after a while. Portuguese *telenovelas* (soap operas) are excellent for this. The language used is generally of the everyday type and you can usually follow the simple plots and story lines with ease. Most films are subtitled in Portugal and not dubbed, so this makes it even better. You can listen to English and read Portuguese.
- Don't worry about making mistakes and being perfect. *Just do it*! You won't learn if you don't make mistakes. Think of how many mistakes you hear when foreigners are trying to learn to

speak English. Do you make fun of them? No. In general most people are appreciative of others making the effort to learn their language. Plus, it can be real fun.

- If someone replies to you in English, just keep speaking Portuguese, or if need be, ask them politely if they would mind not speaking to you in English.
- If you have certain jobs or shopping to do the next day, or later the same day, do a bit of homework before you go out. Make a list of the verbs and vocabulary you might need and learn them and take the list with you for support. Many situations are quite similar, so once you've learnt a few stock phrases you can use them again and again.
- If you forget a word, then remember that you may be able to use a few other words to describe the one you've forgotten and most of the time you will get offered the word, or at least the person you are speaking to will understand you.

CASE STUDY: LUCY PEPPER

When I was 20, I came to Portugal on a field trip as an art student. We spent two weeks in Porto and painted and drew in the city and in some of the vineyards along the length of the Douro. Porto was stinky and decaying, and the Douro unspeakably beautiful. We were fed proper Portuguese food: boiled *bacalhau* (codfish), with olives and chickpeas, and a chicken foot stew that offended the vegetarians' tender hearts. We travelled on a train with open doors; if you were mad enough you could dangle your feet out while you sat on the entrance step. We danced in the grapes with farmhands, whose deluded foreman earlier in the day had been supplying me with tots of *aguardente, moscatel* and port while I painted the hillsides. This was a British art student he was trying to get drunk…

I fell in love with Portugal. I have a sketchbook from that trip with the note "I will live in Portugal one day".

Eight years later, and having totally forgotten that note, I met my Portuguese boyfriend. A couple of years after that, I left London for Portugal with our 10-week-old daughter and a head full of ideas of what Portugal was and what life there would be.

We lived in the village where my boyfriend's family had lived for the past 20 years. Azeitão was about 35 kilometres from Lisbon and 15 from Setúbal, and I assumed it would be the archetypal Portuguese village of the collective British dream. What it is, however, is a sprawling suburb made up of five or six hamlets that have crept together over time and grown exponentially since the 1970s. The central village, Vila Nigeria de Azurite, is still a jewel, albeit a bit of a crusty jewel with the edges knocked off, but much of the rest of the area is characterless 'burb populated by those drawn by the fashionable fame the area has mysteriously gained. If you squint, you can still see the splendour of the place.

After 10 years, we moved into a hamlet four kilometres away, inside the Parque Natural, which *is* the Portuguese village of our dreams. We've been here a year and are just about to fix the place up and steeling ourselves for all the dealings with the council.

I arrived in 1999 with 'Learn Portuguese in Three Months'-level Portuguese. I soon realised that I'd need 'Talk Like a Native'-level Portuguese if I was to defend myself from the mother-in-law. My *sogra* is a hard-working woman with her heart in the right place, but she does like to *help*. Like many Portuguese of a certain generation, whose first exposure to the English consisted of the vacuous rich in Cascais and Estoril of the 1950s, she didn't think an Englishwoman would be capable of much beyond waking mid-morning and ringing the bell for the servant to bring her breakfast. Luckily, I have an ear for languages and it didn't take long to be able to speak Portuguese pretty well. That was the best thing I ever did. Learning the language properly opened up this country for me. I speak Portuguese fluently, and live a totally integrated life in Portugal, spending 50 percent of my time talking, writing and thinking in Portuguese. My kids go to Portuguese schools. I work in Portuguese. The majority of my friends are Portuguese. In fact, it took me five years to meet any other foreigners nearby.

The culture shock and madness of a new country, and no one to share this with, led me to start a blog in 2003, an anonymous one, where I wrote and railed against the insanities of this place. I drew the pictures too. They didn't like that. My fictitious and exaggerated persona quickly became infamous in the Portuguese blogosphere, and known to many as 'that dreadful English woman'. I received many horrified emails of "How *dare* you?", but many more "Oh, God, you're *so* right" from Portuguese readers... And that's how I got back into working again. I had thought the only way I'd ever be able to work as an illustrator again would be to write and illustrate some *Year in Provence* style book, 'quaintifying' a place for Londoners to dream about on cold nights, and hoping the fashion for such books hadn't waned and that I might get it published.

Working in Portugal is tough and the money is rubbish — and there's not much of it for an artist, even though the bar isn't that high. The bureaucracy also sucks, day-to-day life if you're raising kids and trying to work (i.e. living here, not holidaying) can be as stressful as it is in the UK, and life isn't much cheaper. But if you haven't a problem with any of the above, then Portugal *is* paradise on earth.

I have only one piece of coverall advice for anyone moving here: learn the language, properly, and then keep learning it. Read newspapers and books, watch the TV (a bit; it is awful), and make friends beyond your estate agent. This is the only way you'll ever get to really *live* in Portugal and know that its culture is stuck in the past but grasping at the future, that its food can be glorious even if it looks disgusting, and that its people are as lovely, ghastly, intelligent, vain, generous, jealous and funny as the people of anywhere else in the world. If only you'd learn the language, you'd know that.

Lucy Pepper, Azeitão
www.lucypepper.com

The Buying Process At-a-Glance

1. At Home — Planning and Research
2. In Portugal — Research Trip
3. At Home — Organise Buying Trip
4. In Portugal — Buying Trip
5. Finalise Purchase

Decide Why You're Buying

- ☐ Investment
- ☐ Rental
- ☐ Holidays
- ☐ For family
- ☐ To live

↓

Determine Finance

- ☐ Mortgage/remortgage
- ☐ Staged financing
- ☐ Credit cards
- ☐ Sell something/cash in stocks or options
- ☐ Get financial advice

↓

Do Research

- ☐ Read this book.
- ☐ Check property listings.
- ☐ Check credentials of estate agents, solicitors, builders/developers, architects, etc.
- ☐ Research locations.

↓

Make Criteria

Where? ☐Town/city ☐Countryside ☐Coast ☐Village
Transport? ☐Driving ☐Trains ☐Airports ☐Motorways
Amenities? ☐Hospitals ☐Schools ☐Shops ☐Nightlife
Type? ☐Self-build ☐New build ☐Off-plan ☐Resale

↓

Make Specification

Size? ☐Bedrooms ☐Bathrooms ☐Garage
Outdoor space? ☐Garden ☐Patio/terrace ☐Pool

↓

Arrange Research Trip

- ☐ Flights
- ☐ Accommodation
- ☐ Travel
- ☐ Meetings – agent, vendor, solicitor, builder, etc.

Visit Short–listed Locations

- ☐ Get a feel for the area and properties available.
- ☐ Visit local estate agents.
- ☐ Visit developers/collect details of properties.
- ☐ Meet up with private vendors.
- ☐ Meet solicitors, architects, builders, etc.

repeat as necessary

Check In Point

Is this still what you want to do?
Is this still the right area?
Are your criteria correct?
Is your budget adequate?

Finance

- ☐ Ensure finance is available and accessible.
- ☐ Select bank and make appointment to open account.

Arrange Inspection Trip

- ☐ Flights and accommodation.
- ☐ Travel/car hire.
- ☐ Meetings – estate agents/vendors/developers – send or tell them your criteria and ensure they have properties to match!
- ☐ Meetings – solicitors/builders/architects, etc.

Step 2: In Portugal – Research Trip

Step 3: Back Home – Organise Buying Trip

Viewings With Estate Agents/Vendors/Developers

- ☐ Be clear on criteria.
- ☐ Take trusted translator (if you need one).
- ☐ Take camera and video camera – take lots of photos and video footage to help you decide later.
- ☐ Make notes & use property check list in appendix.

↓

Make Short List

- ☐ Compare each property against original criteria.
- ☐ Reject any obvious properties.
- ☐ Revisit the properties alone – at different times!
- ☐ Say 'Hi' to the neighbours and find out local gossip.
- ☐ Check out local amenities.
- ☐ Do your own checks – Is the paperwork correct? Who owns it? Can you do renovations? Is the property structurally sound? etc

↓

Check In Point

Does the vendor own the house?
Does the agent have a valid AMI Nº?
Does the developer have a valid Alvará Nº?
Does the solicitor have valid Cédula Nº?

↓

Buy Property

- ☐ Searches, surveys and promissory contract drawn up.
- ☐ Engage solicitor/translator/surveyor/builder.
- ☐ Sign promissory contract and pay deposit.
- ☐ Get certified copies of documents and IDs to present to notary and proof that IMT has been paid.
- ☐ Sign final deed and pay balance (12-18 weeks approx).
- ☐ Property registered at land registry.
- ☐ Receive certified copies of all documents and change of utility contracts.

Off-Plan, New-Build, Resale or Self-Build

People have many different requirements and tastes when it comes to buying property and certain approaches may suit you better than others. In order to help you choose the right approach, I've provided a list of the pros and cons for each type of build. There may be some overlap between off-plan and new-build, depending at what stage you are buying these types of properties.

Off-Plan

Pros:

- ✓ You will be moving into a brand new property with brand new fittings.
- ✓ You can usually choose your own bathroom suites, kitchen, tiles, paint, heating systems and other fittings.
- ✓ You may be able to alter some things at the design stage, such as an interior room layout, subject to planning permission via the architect.
- ✓ If one of several properties on a complex, you will get a better choice if you buy early on, e.g. size, shape, design, views, etc.
- ✓ In most cases, you are buying at a discount, that is, the price of the property you are buying at now will be

less than it would be if already built. This is usually due to the developer wanting to attract investors to help finance the construction. Some people even sell the property on before completion to make a profit.

- ✓ Stage payments allow you to spread the cost of your purchase.
- ✓ You will get a five-year warranty against structural defects on completion.

Cons:

- ✗ The builder could go bust and you will be left with an unfinished property.
- ✗ The builder could go bust after your property is finished and, therefore, it could be left on an unfinished development/urbanisation.
- ✗ The communal areas are often the last to be finished and, therefore, it could be hard to rent out the property for quite some time, should you wish to do so.
- ✗ If the project is in its early stages or it overruns (which projects invariably do) then you could be waiting for quite some time before moving in and/or renting it out.
- ✗ Building work could still be continuing around you for some time after you move in and the dust, dirt and noise that goes with it. Once again this could affect its rental potential early on.

- ✗ If you buy in the early stages or before construction has even started, then you may not have a true idea of what it will really end up looking like.

New-Build

Pros:

- ✓ The property is completely finished and you can move in straight away.
- ✓ If on an existing development, the infrastructure and facilities are likely to be in place.
- ✓ The building work in the area is usually finished and, therefore, it is quieter, cleaner and easier to rent the property.
- ✓ You will have a five-year warranty against structural defects.
- ✓ It is less likely that the property will have any of the maintenance issues that you might have with an older property.
- ✓ The fittings will be new.

Cons:

- ✗ Newer properties tend to have less land and are more likely to be on a development or urbanisation, which you may not like.
- ✗ The property is less likely to have the charm or character of an older one.

× You will have had no input on the choice of fittings unless you have agreed to buy it before it has been fully completed.

Resale

Pros:

✓ The property is completely finished and you can move in straight away. Therefore, less waiting time.

✓ You can negotiate on the price a lot more.

✓ If on a development, the infrastructure and facilities are likely to be well established.

✓ If the property has gardens, they are also likely to be well established.

✓ You can see exactly what you are getting and most problems will have been resolved.

✓ Older properties are more likely to have character and charm and also more land.

✓ More varied choice and availability.

Cons:

× There will be no builder's warranty, if older than five years.

× There might be more maintenance issues and renovation works to do, especially on older properties.

× More variability in prices with some owners holding out for well over the market value for their properties.

Self-Build

Pros:

- ✓ You can choose the plot where you wish to have your home built.
- ✓ While, of course, having to abide by the local planning regulations, you will have complete freedom to design your house.
- ✓ You can select the architect and builder of your choice and choose all the materials and fittings.
- ✓ You can be a lot more involved in the building process from start to finish.
- ✓ Stage payments allow you to spread the cost of your purchase.
- ✓ Everything will be brand new and tailor-made.
- ✓ You will get a five-year warranty against structural defects on completion.

Cons:

- ✗ 'Red tape' and general overbearing bureaucracy in Portugal, which at times might leave you exasperated and frustrated.
- ✗ A long waiting time for each stage to be completed and until you can finally move in.
- ✗ Choosing an unreliable architect and/or builder, or those whose working methods you turn out not to like.

- ✖ If you are not in the country, you will need to employ a project manager to keep an eye on progress.
- ✖ The builder could go bust and you will be left with an unfinished property.
- ✖ Costs can easily escalate and deadlines can slip without careful and consistent project management.

Location

One of the biggest regrets people, especially permanent residents, have in relation to buying property in Portugal is that they chose the wrong location.

Choosing the right location for your needs is essential and must be very carefully considered.

As previously discussed in the *Relocating* chapter, those wishing to buy a property as a holiday home, or those wishing to buy to let, will often have completely different needs from those looking to permanently relocate.

Those of retirement age may also have different requirements in comparison to younger couples with children, who may need to work.

In order to help you decide, I have provided a list of the pros and cons for each type of location. However, please bear in mind that this is a general list and that in Portugal there is often little difference between what constitutes a small town and a large village.

As with anything in life, it is always best to experience things for yourself.

Countryside

Pros:

- ✓ Peace and tranquillity.
- ✓ No hustle and bustle.
- ✓ Freedom and privacy to do as you wish.
- ✓ Self-sufficiency is possible.
- ✓ Closer to nature and nice scenery.
- ✓ Cheaper to buy than in coastal or city locations.
- ✓ Often lots of land and larger sized properties.
- ✓ Less crime.

Cons:

- × Car is essential to go anywhere and a back up car might also required in case one breaks down.
- × Often further away from the nearest shops, bars, restaurants, amenities and medical services.
- × Poor (if any) public transport.
- × Bad roads: narrow, sometimes hilly with poor surfaces.
- × Poor or no utility services.
- × Climate extremes: hotter in the summer and colder in the winter, often with strong winds, if on a hilltop.
- × Fires more likely.
- × Solitude, remoteness and loneliness.

- × Harder to rent out and sell than coastal/city property.
- × Unlikely to find work locally.
- × Harder to maintain land and property, as well as more costly.

Villages

Pros:

- ✓ Neighbours around to help if you have a problem.
- ✓ Community spirit once you've been accepted into the village.
- ✓ More likely to experience the 'real' Portugal.
- ✓ Small shops, bars, restaurants, minor services and amenities.
- ✓ Public transport to the nearest town (although may be quite sporadic).
- ✓ Cheaper to buy than in coastal or city locations.
- ✓ Less crime.

Cons:

- × Villagers less likely to speak English, so you will need to learn Portuguese in order to fully integrate.
- × Often takes a long time to be fully accepted into the community and people tend to want to know your business.
- × Poor utility services.
- × Harder to rent out than coastal/city property.

- ✗ Less likely to find work locally.
- ✗ If you have children they may have to travel to the nearest town for school, and for the elderly and infirm it may be too far from medical services.

Coast

Pros:

- ✓ Sea breeze helps make the summer heat more bearable.
- ✓ Usually reliable public transport.
- ✓ Good utility services.
- ✓ Close to shops, bars, restaurants, amenities and medical services.
- ✓ Entertainment and nightlife, especially in the summer.
- ✓ More likely to find English speakers.
- ✓ Easier to sell.
- ✓ Easier to rent out, especially in the summer.
- ✓ Easier to find work.

Cons:

- ✗ Can be a ghost town in the winter when many businesses close for their annual break.
- ✗ Parking problems and traffic congestion in the summer.
- ✗ Noise from holidaymakers, bars, restaurants and traffic in the summer.

- ✗ Overcrowded beaches, and packed restaurants and bars in the summer.
- ✗ Property is more expensive to buy.
- ✗ More crime.

Towns & Cities

Pros:

- ✓ Close to all kinds of businesses, shops, bars, restaurants, amenities and medical services.
- ✓ Entertainment, culture and nightlife.
- ✓ More likely to find English speakers.
- ✓ Good public transport.
- ✓ Good utility services.
- ✓ Easier to rent out, especially long-term.
- ✓ Easier to find work.

Cons:

- ✗ Noise from neighbours, pedestrians and traffic.
- ✗ Parking problems and traffic congestion.
- ✗ No community spirit.
- ✗ Lack of green spaces.
- ✗ Expensive to buy.
- ✗ Small plot sizes and properties.
- ✗ More crime.
- ✗ More hustle and bustle, and possibly stress.

CASE STUDY: EMMA CRABTREE

I'm Emma Crabtree and I live in Condeixa-a-Velha, Central Portugal, with my husband Lawrence. We have been in Portugal since 2004.

We originally relocated from our one-bedroom townhouse in South London to a large, detached house in a small and typical Portuguese village in the Beira Litoral, where we were the only English speaking couple. We'd both made lists of towns we'd like to live in or close to and Coimbra, which is our district capital, was the only place that had made it onto both our lists! We knew that Portugal was where we wanted to live many, many years ago. I would say that the planning and preparation we did before leaving London has been the key to our success. We knew the country, the systems and the bureaucracy well before making the final commitment of buying a property. My first tip would be *plan ahead* – do your research and make contingency plans.

The house we bought was advertised through local agents and we viewed it, and many others, while we were in Portugal for two weeks during Euro 2004. Although we had researched and viewed other properties through expat agents, this company had properties that met our budget and ticked more boxes than any other agent. We bought through our lawyer, acting with power of attorney, and moved in September. Although the house came only partly furnished, we didn't take our furniture from the UK. This was a mistake as there isn't the choice available in Portugal as there is in the UK. Furniture and white goods can be very expensive and there are very few second-hand stores along the high street. No Oxfam, Help the Aged or RSPCA stores here!

Our honeymoon period didn't last long. The summer extended into mid-October, and then it rained and rained. There's a reason Portugal is so green and has such a wonderful diversity of flora and fauna! And the winter was bitterly cold. Our house did not have central heating and we only installed a fireplace in late November, by which time friends had been to visit and froze most of the time. This cycle of glorious summers followed by wet and very cold winters has continued throughout our time in Portugal. So my second tip would be to ensure you have some sort of central heating in your home, wherever you end up. You won't use it from April to October, but you *will* need it at some stage!

The neighbours couldn't have been more generous, welcoming and kind and we have made friends who will be with us for life. I had read that the Portuguese are embarrassed about their way of living and won't take you into their homes. Not our villagers! We lunched and dined with our new neighbours within six weeks of moving in and were forever having people over for coffee. In hindsight, however, the village wasn't right for us. You can take the girl out of the city (15 years working and breathing London life), but can you take the city out of the girl? Our village had no facilities and the nearest supermarket was a 20-minute drive away. I was isolated and felt lonely. My third tip, therefore, is to know oneself. Are you absolutely sure that being in a remote, albeit gorgeous, stone cottage, alone, with snowed-in roads is for you?

It was at this time that I started my business, Red Box Virtual Office. Initially this was to give me something to do and to provide us with an income. Neither of us are near to retirement age and gardening can only take up so much of your time, especially over the winter. I'm what is known as a virtual assistant and my clients have been based in the US, Middle East, UK, Europe and Australia. The majority of my tasks are administration based: client care, customer service, sourcing and procurement, email management and so on. The tasks may vary, but what I fundamentally do never changes: I provide individuals and small businesses with support when they need it most. From starting off providing spreadsheets for my mum, I now run a small, but perfectly functional company for entrepreneurs and small businesses who are based somewhere other than in Condeixa-a-Velha.

There were several reasons for moving from our village. Not least of which was that I couldn't rely on the telephone or electricity service and these are very important utilities to have when running an online business. We were fortunate to advertise and sell our house within four months.

Since that time, we have bought two further properties, one of which we renovated and where we are living now; the other we sold. Our new house is well located for Red Box; Coimbra is just a 10-minute drive away and the A1 connects me with Porto and Lisbon within an hour or so. I achieve so much more now – including networking, lunches and dinners – and have begun to attract Portuguese businesses too. I would recommend thinking about what you can do to earn a living, or at least fill your days, if you are relocating and under the age of 70. What transferable skills do you have? What work experience? Lawrence is now a trained TEFL teacher, but his background is in social housing. Unemployment is high here, even among the well trained and qualified, and the cost of living is not as cheap as it used to be. Your nest egg will be nibbled away by all those *pastel de nata* (custard tart) stops you make each week.

One of the reasons new immigrants find themselves in difficulty is because they have bought a property without being able to speak the language and without independent advice. I'd highly recommend taking language classes (my fourth tip) both before relocating and once you are settled in Portugal. We took classes before, during and after our move, culminating at the University of Coimbra. It is frequently remarked by my Portuguese friends that the English, or indeed other nationalities, don't speak Portuguese and it annoys and frustrates them. Couple this with the fact that the majority of council employees you will have to deal with in small towns won't speak English, and you will see why being able to understand and be understood is crucial.

Portugal is a country of contradictions and I liken it to the UK in the 1960s. It is an incredibly beautiful country, but littering and roadside dumping are rife. The Portuguese adore children, but their attitude towards animals (abandoning them or not having them neutered) is backward. There's live bull fighting on the TV and villagers will butcher their own livestock. Portuguese women will smoke and drink through their pregnancies and take their babies into smoky bars, and there are jobsworths wherever you go. These are all issues that you need to take on board before moving to Portugal.

Third property lucky; we are happy in our small, bijou house with its enormous garden and great neighbours. We can walk to bars and restaurants and have all the amenities you may need on our doorstep. The Portuguese way of life, though it can be incredibly frustrating, suits us. It's not a stress-free life – anyone who has to deal with the local finance office will tell you that – but we are incredibly fortunate to have found somewhere we both feel comfortable and welcomed.

Emma Crabtree,
Condeixa-a-Velha, Central Portugal
www.redboxvirtualoffice.com

Regions of Portugal

For the purpose of this property buying guide I have divided Portugal into five main regions:

- North
- Centre
- Lisbon
- Alentejo
- Algarve

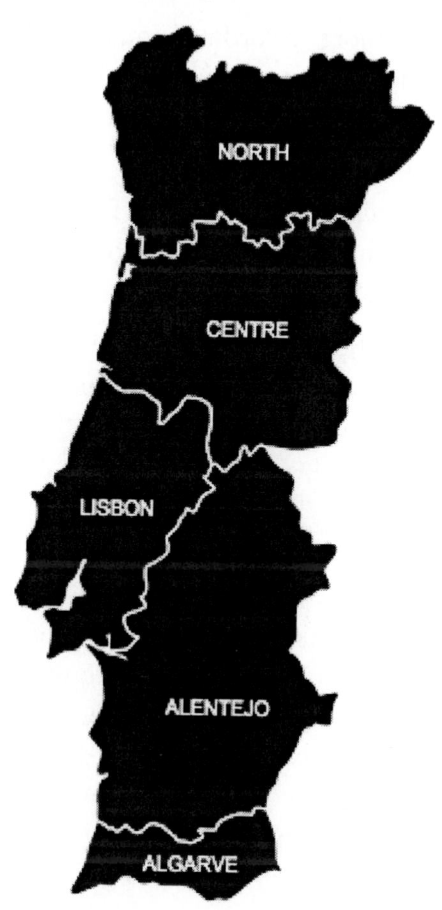

North

Not everyone who is thinking of relocating abroad is looking for endless hours of heat and sunshine. In fact, many people don't enjoy the extreme summer temperatures that can be found in some parts of Southern Europe. If you simply want a different and much more affordable and laidback lifestyle, then Northern Portugal might just be the answer.

The North consists of the Costa Verde (Green Coast), which is situated in the northwest and includes the provinces of Minho and the Douro coast, and part of the Montanhas (Mountains) in the northeast known as Trás-os-Montes.

The Minho borders the Galician province of Spain and it is often said that it bears more of a resemblance to its Spanish neighbour than Portugal. They both share some Celtic customs and there is a slight blurring of accents, for example the Portuguese in this area pronounce the letter 'v' as a 'b' as in Spain.

It is the greenest part of Portugal, mainly due to the large amount of rainfall in the region. The countryside is lush with rolling hills and mountains, woods and pine forests, fertile valleys and vineyards, and there are many unspoilt, long, sandy beaches and quiet coves. The landscape is like a patchwork quilt of small farms and houses, and there are some very beautiful stately homes and mansions, as well as ancient castles dotted about.

The Minho hasn't changed much in hundreds of years and is still a very conservative, rural and traditional region. In fact, you can still see oxen pulling carts to plough fields. Similarly, Trás-os-Montes, the most backward and poorest province in Portugal, seems to be lost in a medieval time warp with people washing their clothes in streams and some homes without mains electricity.

Three rivers can be found in the region: the Rio Lima, the Rio Minho (which forms the border with Spain) and the Rio Douro.

A wine known as *vinho verde* (green wine) is produced in the Minho, and in Porto, Portugal's second largest city, the famous *vinho do Porto* (Port wine) is made.

The main cities and towns in this region are Braga, Bragança, Chaves, Guimarães, Porto, Viana do Castelo and Vila Real.

The region is home to some of the most impressive historic centres in Portugal. Guimarães is the birthplace of the country and the beautiful Ponte de Lima is a regular host to the finance ministers of Europe. The spectacular national parks (Peneda Gerês in particular) contain many areas of protected wildlife and there are even wolves still residing in the mountains.

The famous, Portuguese cockerel symbol was born in Barcelos in this region and dates back to a 14th Century legend.

Portugal's longest motorway, the A1, which goes from Lisbon to Porto, enters this region and then connects with the A3 towards Braga. There is also a coastal road, which goes through Vila do Conde until Valença.

As well as the improved road networks in the region, there are good railway links to both Porto and Vigo across the border in Spain, and with regular flights to Porto from the UK and an airport at Vigo less than an hour's drive away, access to the region from other parts of Europe has never been better. This is with the exception of Trás-os-Montes, which has a rather poor road network and a limited public transport system.

Northern Portugal has seen little in the way of tourism, but visitors are increasing year on year. Viana do Castelo, the largest and main town in Minho province, is known as the folklore capital and is an attraction to outsiders for its many festivals, especially in the summer months. Much of the coastal area between Porto and Caminha is also now showing signs of holiday developments.

Many surfers prefer the challenges of the Atlantic Ocean further north and there are a large number of other water sports enjoyed, for example canoeing and boating. Climbing, hiking and fishing are also popular throughout the whole region.

The climate in the Costa Verde area is very damp and more akin to Northern Europe and certainly less reliable than more southerly parts of Portugal. However, the summers can still be very warm and pleasant, and many people prefer the beauty of the unspoilt countryside and fresh air to the more brown, arid and occasionally oppressive south.

Being mountainous, Trás-os-Montes is naturally more extreme in climatic conditions and can have particularly long, cold winters. Locals have been known to refer to the weather as "nine months of winter and three months of hell!"

More and more foreign buyers are now coming to Northern Portugal for its quality of life. However, property prices are quite expensive compared to the central area of Portugal. This is due to the fact that many Portuguese emigrants still retain houses in the region, as well as those that work in Lisbon who own weekend or holiday homes.

While the Minho is generally expensive, there are pockets that are cheaper as you move inland towards Monção, and up into the mountains. Some mountain villages, even as close as Arcos de Valdevez, can also be less expensive although perhaps still not quite as cheap as the central region. It would seem that the prices vary across the northern part of Portugal more than in other parts and naturally, those areas in which people want to live are more expensive than those which are more remote.

Porto has a fair number of foreigners, including British expatriates working in the Port wine industry and some teaching English as a foreign language. However, the large-scale emigration by Portuguese in this region perhaps gives some indication as to the likely employment opportunities.

Outside of Porto, the region is very poor and employment prospects bleak. As an expat, your chances of finding any sort of work are close to zero. Therefore, this is really a region for retirees or those with alternative income.

In general, there are more rural farmhouses and town property for sale, as opposed to new builds. Ruins or dilapidated old manor houses and tumbledown granite cottages are also available for renovation, especially in rural areas, as due to the large-scale emigration by local people over the years, a lot of properties have been left to fall into disrepair.

The region is ripe for investment and there is a fairly active property market, especially for renovation projects. Golfing and leisure resorts have also started to make their mark in the last couple of years, as well as some small-scale developments. However, due to strict planning restrictions in the region and many areas of protected status, it is unlikely that mass developments will emerge.

Areas in particular to watch out for are around Valença, Viana do Castelo, Modelo do Minho, Ponte de Lima and

Ponte da Barca, and in general along the Lima and Minho Valleys.

Centre

The central region includes the provinces of Beira Alta, Beira Baixa and Beira Litoral. The Serra da Estrela, the highest mountains in Portugal, divide the Beira Alta and Beira Baixa.

This central area also includes what has become known as the Costa de Prata (Silver Coast). The name deriving from the fact that the sun's reflection on the sea gives a silvery light. It stretches from Porto down to Lisbon along the Atlantic coastline.

This region is probably the most diverse in Portugal with its rolling hills, wooded mountain areas, spectacular scenery, pine and eucalyptus trees, varied flora and fauna, and long, sandy beaches. It also has many unspoilt, little fishing towns and coastal villages and rural inland towns and villages. The region is also known for its many sites of historic, religious and architectural importance. It has two main rivers: the Rio Zêzere and Rio Mondego.

The main cities and towns in this region are: Aveiro, Caldas da Rainha, Castelo Branco, Coimbra, Leiria, Guarda, Óbidos, Tomar and Viseu. Other towns of note are Alcobaça, Batalha, Fátima, Figueira do Foz, Foz do Arelho, Nazaré, Peniche and São Martinho do Porto.

Coimbra is the university town of Portugal and has one of the oldest universities in continuous operation in Europe, founded in the 13th Century.

Since the A8 motorway was opened a few years ago, thereby reducing the drive from Lisbon's airport to under an hour, the region has really been opened up and in the last few years has seen an explosion in foreign property buying, especially around the Óbidos area.

Porto's Francisco Sá Carneiro airport is also used by those residing in the more northern areas of this central region.

The A1 motorway passes close to Coimbra and the IP5 links Spain to Aveiro. There is also work underway on the IC9 motorway, which links Tomar to the Costa de Prata. This will reduce the driving time to the coast (Marinha Grande) to around 25 to 30 minutes.

The region is well served by major roads. However, you will find that the further from the beaten path you venture, the poorer the quality of the roads become. The road surfaces in some of the more remote and rural areas are often uneven, with lots of sharp bends and hills.

Another point worth noting is the approval of the IC3 extension. This will affect a lot of properties in Central Portugal and is something you should be aware of and get thoroughly checked out if looking for a property in this area. It will start from the existing IC3 north of

Tomar and link up to Coimbra, making the EN110 road a secondary route. It is due to take five to seven years to complete.

A reasonably good and inexpensive train service operates between many larger towns in Central Portugal and both Lisbon and the North. There is also a high-speed rail link between Aveiro and Salamanca in Central Spain in the pipeline.

As well as good transport links, the increasing popularity of Central Portugal has been due to its cheaper property prices in comparison to those of the more famous Algarve coastal region. However, with this increasing popularity there has no doubt been some rise in prices and there can be quite a variation depending on what part of Central Portugal you wish to purchase in.

Moving inland, areas such as Tomar (a UNESCO world heritage site) and Abrantes situated near the beautiful Castelo do Bode (Portugal's second biggest reservoir) have become more and more popular for both holiday homes and permanent residence. The area has rolling hills, rivers and a plethora of quaint villages and towns to visit.

The Castelo do Bode lake, which spans 60 kilometres, not only contains an abundance of wild life, but is very popular for water sports, such as canoeing, fishing, scuba diving and water skiing, and there is demand from both the domestic market and from overseas buyers for properties close to the lake.

Despite the tightening of planning rules adjacent to water sources, such as rivers, lakes and reservoirs, making them more at a premium, it is still possible to purchase a reasonably priced home in the vicinity.

Many other social activities can be enjoyed in the Tomar and Abrantes areas and they also offer great facilities, services and amenities. Therefore, property prices tend to be slightly more expensive than areas found a little further north, such as in Penela, Lousã, Mirando do Corvo and Arganil.

These more northerly areas, while having stunning scenery and still being very popular, are more remote and do not have as many services and amenities. Therefore, you would have to weigh up the pros and cons, as well as your priorities.

Tomar now has a sizeable expat community and while not overly touristy you will perhaps find more English speakers than in the more remote areas in this region. This might help with your transition into Portugal if lack of proficiency in the language is a cause for concern and if you are thinking of any possible expat orientated business.

However, as with nearly all the regions in Portugal, employment is not at all easy to come by, so make sure you do your homework first if you need to make a living.

Tourism in Central Portugal has developed rapidly, especially on the Costa de Prata, and it is now a strong alternative to the Algarve. This might also be an important consideration if you are hoping to get any rental income from your property.

While the climate is mild, it should be noted that the Atlantic waves tend to be fiercer (a surfer's paradise) and the water and air temperatures a few degrees cooler than in the Algarve.

The climate is quite variable in Central Portugal with the more northerly areas often being substantially colder during the winter, especially the nearer you get to the mountains. In fact, skiing and other winter sports are popular in the Serra da Estrela. Therefore, one has to consider the cost of heating against the price of a cheaper property in the long-term.

The cost of living can be cheaper in Central Portugal than, for example the Algarve and Lisbon. However, if you shop in the main supermarkets and chains, there will not be such a marked difference.

The region is very popular with expats wishing to adopt self-sufficiency, eco and alternative lifestyles and perhaps lends itself better to this than other parts of Portugal.

The property in this region is varied depending on your taste and budget and includes new builds on new developments, plots, seafront apartments, fishermen's cottages, resale properties in the towns and farmhouses or ruins for renovation in the more inland, rural areas.

Central Portugal also has a number of golf courses and some property development in connection to this has already taken place, especially around Óbidos and the Costa de Prata area, for example Bom Sucesso; a resort, leisure, golf and spa, Quinta de Óbidos; a country club and equestrian centre with luxury lakeside villas and Royal Óbidos; a spa and golf resort with both villas and apartments.

Lisbon

Lisbon includes not only the capital itself, but also the southern parts of Estremadura and Ribatejo provinces. It stretches from Ericeira in the north to near Sines in the south.

Going west along the coast there are many stylish resorts, such as Estoril and Cascais with their top hotels, casino, big villas and nice beaches.

Inland to the northwest of these resorts and up into the hills, is Sintra (a UNESCO world heritage town) with its lush, green woodlands, breathtaking views, beautiful gothic 'fairy tale' buildings and Moorish legacy.

To the south of the Rio Tejo (River Tagus) is Caparica and the Costa Azul (Blue Coast) with its largely unspoilt, long, sandy beaches and sheltered at the southern end of the peninsula by the Serra da Arrábida Mountains.

Outside of Lisbon, Sintra, Cascais and Estoril, other towns of note in the region are Mafra, Setúbal, Sesimbra and Torres Vedras.

Lisbon is steeped in history and culture, and due to the fact that it is built on seven hills, it has amazing views wherever you go.

Lisbon is a small capital by European standards and is a city of total contrasts. From the quaint Alfama district (the oldest part of the city) with its narrow streets and rattling trams, the historic Moorish Castelo de São Jorge (St George Castle) overlooking the city, and the many funiculars and elevators to the Expo area with its modern architecture and restaurants, the trendy Chiado and Bairro Alto districts with their cafés, bars and nightlife and the impressive Vasco da Gama and 25 de Abril (25th April) bridges spanning the Rio Tejo.

Despite its quaint, old-fashioned charms, some parts of Lisbon are very dilapidated and in dire need of renovation and repair. This is mainly due to the tight building restrictions, bureaucracy and archaic rental laws. However, efforts are now being made to change this and clean up the city's fading façades and structures.

The climate in this region tends to be a little cooler than the Algarve in the summer, largely due to the stronger westerly breezes off of the Atlantic. It also tends to be quite a bit colder and damper in the winter. However, by Northern European standards it is still fairly mild and is one of the warmest European capitals all year round.

The sea is never far away and with a variety of beaches to choose from — the long, sandy Caparica coast or the more rugged Guincho and Praia Grande, for instance — it is a popular destination for those who love water sports, especially surfing, windsurfing and kite surfing.

Sintra has its own microclimate due to its hilly, but near coastal position and is often used as a getaway from the city down below during the long, hot summer months.

Lisbon has an excellent road network and public transport system, as one would expect with it being the capital city. Overground trains, trams, buses, ferries and a metro (underground) are all fairly cheap and reliable.

However, it does have very bad traffic and parking problems and it is only recently that the Lisbon authorities have considered building more car parks and insisted on underground parking being a requirement for all new buildings.

A proposal to create an infrastructure at Alcochete (south of Lisbon) to complement and take some of the strain off of Lisbon's rather old and outgrown Portela airport (known as the Portela+1 formula) is in the pipeline with the idea being to transfer some of the low-cost flights to this modular airport.

A high-speed rail link between Lisbon and Madrid in Spain should also be completed by 2013.

Most foreign buyers in this area tend to be those who are working in the capital, but there is also now a sizeable proportion buying second homes and relocating for other reasons, including retirement.

More multi-national companies are now in evidence in Lisbon, making employment prospects possible for many expats. However, it is still not an easy task to land a job and teaching English as a foreign language is really only one of the very few other options.

While property in Lisbon tends to be some of the most expensive in Portugal, it is still relatively cheap compared to many other European cities, and is, in fact, one of the more affordable capitals in Western Europe.

Popular areas are: Alcântara, Alfama, Bairro Alto, Belém, Bica, Campo de Ourique, Castelo, Chiado, Graça, Lapa, Principe Real, Rato and Santa Catarina.

The range of property is diverse. You can find traditional city apartments with character in Alfama, Castelo and Graça, modern riverfront flats and penthouses at Parque de Nações in the Expo area, sleek apartments in Chiado and family homes and even palaces in Lapa.

Other areas of choice for expats are along the 'Linha de Cascais' (also referred to as the Estoril Riviera) where you will find bigger houses with gardens, perhaps more suitable for family life in comparison to city centre apartments.

Sintra is another popular area and offers everything from country houses, castles, palaces, estates and villas to smaller village houses and apartments.

In order to find cheaper property and affordable renovation projects in this region, places north of Lisbon – Torres Vedras or south of the Rio Tejo near to Sesimbra and the Serra da Arrábida, for example – may offer what you are looking for.

However, it should be noted that in the southern half of the Setúbal Peninsula, which includes Azeitão, Palmela, Sesimbra, Quinta do Conde and Setúbal itself, the larger mansion houses with land are rather expensive and tend to stay in families for years, and there are far fewer of the types of ruins that you might find in Central Portugal and elsewhere.

The building regulations also tend to be very strict in this area with little scope for extending what is already there, and due to the Parque Natural the recent building boom south of Lisbon stops abruptly at this boundary.

Likewise, renovating older properties in Central Lisbon might prove to be somewhat difficult due to the very tight planning restrictions and an overbearing amount of red tape. While you can often change a property internally without too much of a problem, changing a façade will prove a totally different matter and in some cases, it will be impossible.

Long-term renting out of your property, if bought for investment purposes, is also easier in Lisbon than many other parts of Portugal, and while not as popular as the Algarve or Costa de Prata there are some prospects for holiday rentals along the Caparica coast, as well as the Costa Azul and Sintra.

However, your market is much more likely to be native Portuguese, than foreign. Outside of the 'Linha de Cascais' and Sintra there are relatively few expats, with just a scattering of British, German and Dutch and certainly no 'expat enclaves' or British cafés and shops.

One last, but major consideration if you are thinking of living south of the Rio Tejo, is that if you have to travel into Central Lisbon in the rush hour it will take you a very long time indeed. The bridges are notoriously jammed at peak hours and you will have to pay tolls to cross.

Alentejo

The Alentejo region is situated from the Rio Tejo (River Tagus) in the north until the Algarve in the south. It borders Spain in the East and the Atlantic in the West and includes the provinces of Alto Alentejo, Baixo Alentejo and most of Ribatejo.

The region covers nearly a third of Portugal and is the largest but least populated. It is characterised by its rolling hilly grasslands and wheat fields, wide-open spaces, vast agricultural estates, whitewashed villages and walled towns with castles and hilltop forts.

The Alentejo also has many cork oak forests, numerous olive trees, fields of sunflowers, beautiful flora and fauna and is known for its horse and bull breeding. It has often been referred to as the 'bread basket' of Portugal.

Wine production is famous in this region with many wine *quintas* (farms) producing award-winning wines, such as *Esperão*.

The main cities and towns in this region are: Beja, Elvas, Estremoz, Évora, Monsaraz, Moura, Portalegre, Sines and Vila Viçosa.

Unless on the coast, where the Atlantic breezes help moderate the temperature, this is an extremely hot part of Portugal during the summer with temperatures often surpassing 40°C. Conversely, in the winter it is often very cold with temperatures close to freezing at night. The sea is also a little colder along the west coast in comparison to the Algarve.

Now that the A2 motorway extends throughout the Baixo Alentejo into the Algarve, access to the lower part of this region is a lot quicker and easier. There is also a new road being built between Beja and Sines.

The road network is reasonable in the Alentejo, but the public transport system is generally poor. However, the *intercidade* (inter-city) train service between the Algarve and Lisbon stops at Funcheira, Grândola and Alcácer do Sal in this region.

Until fairly recently, the Alentejo has been somewhere that people have mostly driven through on the way to somewhere else, and of little interest to foreign property buyers. This is with the exception of more adventurous types and those looking for complete peace and solitude.

However, this is slowly changing and the Alentejo is rapidly becoming an area of interest for those wishing to be away from the busier Algarve coast and who are looking for substantially cheaper property.

Compared to the rest of Portugal (and certainly many other parts of Europe), prices in the Alentejo are relatively low. However, with the opening of a new airport at Beja, due in April 2011, making it a lot easier to travel to the region, prices are sure to rise and it could well become the next property boom area in Portugal.

As an expat, work in this part of Portugal is going to be very hard to find and unless you have some form of alternative income or are retired, you may well struggle.

Some have found a niche offering painting, horse riding, cycling and hiking/walking holidays and if on the coast, then there may well be a market for renting, especially to Portuguese nationals from Lisbon and the North. You will generally find less English speakers here, in comparison to the Algarve or Lisbon.

Tourism has gradually been increasing over the years with many Portuguese and overseas visitors now heading to the unspoilt Alentejo coastline rather than the busier Algarve.

The more desolated coastline is also very popular with surfers and the region as a whole is attractive to those who like outdoor pursuits. Other activities of interest include bird watching, wine tasting and visiting sites of historical and cultural importance, for example Évora, a UNESCO world heritage site.

There is a large range of property in this region, from coastal apartments along the west coast, which stretches from the border with the Algarve to the Costa Azul (Blue Coast) south of Lisbon, to ruins for renovation, farmhouses, village properties, plots to build and brand new villas with pools. Properties in inland Alentejo are also likely to have a lot more land than in other parts of Portugal.

Golf developments are now starting to feature prominently in the region with the Troia Resort up and running and a new resort at Pinheirinho on the Northern Alentejo coast due for completion in 2012. It will be of low-density construction, and will host golf, leisure and holiday facilities.

Another five areas along the west coast are also earmarked for development, and there is the impressive Parque do Redondo at Lake Vigia between Évora and the Spanish border, as well as the Herdade do Gizo estate in Cuba, which is set to become a horse lover's dream.

However, with many protected areas in this region, especially along the coastline, it is unlikely to become too overdeveloped and hopefully will manage to retain its beauty and charm for those preferring a quieter and more remote existence.

The Alentejo could well be a future destination of choice for many.

Algarve

The Algarve is the most southern region of Portugal and is also a province in its own right.

The word Algarve comes from the Arabic, *Al Gharb* meaning 'The West' and everywhere you look you can still see the Moorish influences in the architecture, for this was the last region of Portugal to be re-conquered.

Whitewashed houses with Moorish chimneys, traditional fishing villages, long, sandy beaches and coves and cliffs characterise this region, together with its hilly countryside dotted with almond, fig, olive, carob and citrus fruit trees. The Algarve also has a range of mountains called the Serra de Monchique, which border Alentejo.

A lot of the Algarve has now become quite built up along the coastline with some over development certainly in evidence. In the summer some of the resorts are bustling and somewhat over crowded.

However, if you travel to the far east and west of the region, as well as only a little way inland, you can still find more typical and unspoilt areas and those that disparage it as not being 'real' Portugal are somewhat misinformed.

Protected areas of natural beauty still exist in this region, with many nature reserves and a particularly wild and rugged western coastline. Surfing, walking, cycling, fishing, bird watching, and of course, golf are activities especially enjoyed throughout the Algarve.

The climate in the Algarve is mild nearly all year round and boasts over 3000 hours of sunshine a year. During the peak summer months temperatures can get very hot, especially inland, where it can be similar to the Alentejo. However, along the coast there is usually a cooling sea breeze, especially the further west you go.

Winters in the Algarve can be damp and chilly and to many people's surprise heating will definitely be required, as night time temperatures can fall quite considerably with occasional frosts.

Sea temperatures, while warmer than other regions of Portugal, can still be quite cold, although travelling east towards Spain will see these temperatures rise a little, as the Mediterranean Sea exerts its influence on the Atlantic Ocean.

The main cities and towns in this region are: Albufeira, Faro, Lagos, Loulé, Olhão, Portimão, Silves, Tavira and Vilamoura.

The A2 motorway was extended a few years ago through Baixo Alentejo and now goes right into the Algarve, where it joins up with the A22. This has made travelling between Lisbon and the Algarve a lot quicker and easier. Other roads in the Algarve are generally good with the A22 motorway going all the way through from west to east and joining up with the Spanish motorway across the border.

Public transport is also adequate in the region and the *Alfa Pendular* and *intercidade* (inter-city) train services between Lisbon and the Algarve are usually very reliable and inexpensive.

Faro airport is now easily accessible from all parts of the Algarve, even the far west, due to the A22 motorway extension and there are many daily budget flights operating from the UK, both charter and schedule.

The Algarve is the region which has always seen the most investment by foreign buyers and is still continuing to do so, largely due to its wonderful climate and laidback lifestyle.

However, due to the expensive price of property now, in comparison to other regions in Portugal, and the fact that for some, it has become a little too developed, it does now have a lot more competition on its hands.

It must be pointed out though that the overdevelopment is all relative and if you compare it with many other seaside destinations, you will find most of the Algarve to be still quite unspoilt.

The recent worldwide recession, which has affected the property market, has also had an impact on the region and although it has perhaps weathered the storm better than its neighbour, Spain, it has still seen a fall in house prices. This means that some properties, out of reach to many just a couple of years back, may now just be affordable, although real bargains may still be hard to come by.

The reasons for people purchasing a property overseas are varied and therefore if the aim is to live permanently in the country for some time and not just for a quick return, then the Algarve will always be attractive to many.

The fact that it is a regular summer holiday favourite and top golfing destination will also help maintain it as a desirable area of Portugal and Europe in which to buy property, especially if one of the aims is to seek rental income.

Since the A22 motorway was extended a few years ago, the largely unspoilt west around Lagos, Luz and beyond, and the west coast has seen a massive surge in development albeit of low-density construction.

The Eastern Algarve, which has traditionally been a little cheaper than central and western parts, has likewise seen development near Tavira and also the Spanish border around Castro Marim and the River Guadiana.

The 'golden triangle' of Vilamoura, Vale do Lobo and Quinta do Lago, where you can find some of the most expensive property in Portugal, if not Europe, is still a big favourite for those with the money to buy there, and many celebrities and sports personalities own property in this area.

The new Formula One track at Portimão in Central Algarve has also now been completed and may entice some for this reason.

If you need to work in Portugal or set up a business, then the Algarve is perhaps the easiest location in which to do so, as a large number of tourist and real estate jobs require English speakers. There is also a substantial English speaking expat community. However, please re-read the *Relocating* chapter as even in the Algarve jobs are not so easy to come by now.

If getting to grips with the Portuguese language is a major issue for you, then this region of Portugal might also be favourable, as a majority of the Algarve population, especially the younger members, speak very good English, as well as often French and German.

You can find every type of property imaginable in the Algarve, from ruins with lots of land in the countryside, to coastal apartments, to new build villas on large developments and, of course, lots of resale property.

CASE STUDY: EMMA BRUNTON

Making an escape from the rat race had been my plan for five years before I left Sydney. I was a film producer, but I had strayed too far away from the film-making and documentaries that had drawn me to the industry in the first place. I was spending my days (and nights too, usually) in the deluded world of television commercials, saving otherwise useless products from obsolescence with a whole lot of window dressing and untruths. I was bored to death in meetings where the ad people ardently argued whether to serve the product sauce with rice or potatoes. Or by standing around at 3 am watching a hamburger on a turntable under a jungle of lights while grown adults pondered if the bun looked soft enough. Was this important? Was it relevant to what was happening in the world? Was this my life?

So when I was fired for refusing to ask a colleague to cancel their holidays (nothing could be more important than finishing a half-made advert), I took it as a blessing. I knew my piggy bank wasn't full yet, but I also knew I might be stuck waiting another five years for the last 20 big ones to appear. It was time to jump in.

I did what had to be done. I sold my entire wardrobe on eBay. I would start my new life naked as a baby with low-cost-airline-approved cabin baggage.

First I went travelling in Asia, and then I visited friends around Europe. That done, I had a long list of countries to visit where I would look for something to do, like opening a café, or having a small hotel, or buying and renovating a house. I had researched some vague scenarios set in Croatia or Bulgaria, on a lake, with free-range chickens.

But first I had to visit Portugal. Years before I had left if off the itinerary of a round-the-Mediterranean trip, because, technically, it's not on the Mediterranean, and I still wanted to go there. I loved the place. I "oo-ed" and "ahh-ed" at the dilapidated architecture of the cities and stuffed my face with pastries. Somehow I could understand what people were saying and Portuguese flowed from my mouth like I had a Babel fish in my ear. I thought the Portuguese were the nicest people in the world. And oh bless! Look at the olive trees and the grape vines and the rows of stone walls... and all those adorable abandoned ruins with 'for sale' signs.

Yes Siree, I was sucked right in. I set myself up in a €15 a night hotel in Lisbon, and every day I'd cross Avenida da Liberdade to spend the day at an internet café in the corner of an 18th-century ballroom. There I researched the property market and found houses I wanted to view. I researched building costs and the cost of living. And most importantly, I investigated what it would take for a non-EU national to get residency in Portugal.

Then I went out and looked at 34 houses. It went on for months. The trouble was, I had seen the house I wanted in the beginning, but the documents for the property were all wrong and the estate agent no help to me. So I kept looking, but never saw another house with the magic of that one. Eventually I came back to it and, with the help of another agent, got the ball rolling on the buying process and the rectification of the deeds.

Then I had to get out of Portugal in order to make my application for a visa. I went and lived in Berlin. Trying to buy a house and making an application for building works is made much harder by being out of the country. The visa process was arduous, with the embassy sending me away repeatedly to get more documentation and testing me to see if I would give up this dream of living in Portugal. It was a difficult time, but I don't regret living in Berlin for a minute because it is where I learned Portuguese. As I don't speak German, group classes weren't an option. I eventually found an English-speaking Brazilian to be my *professora*. I struck gold. She had a real talent for teaching and enormous patience with me, and we became good friends. I had two hours of lessons a day and in six months we had completed an entire school curriculum of grammar. Not only did private lessons keep me focused and enthusiastic, but my teacher helped me talk to the real estate agent, the architect and the embassy when problems got too much for me to handle.

After nine months I had a *projecto de arquitetura*, a *visto de residência* and finally the owner and I were ready to sign an *escritura*. I packed up again and moved back to Portugal. This time I went to live in the small town of Lousã in Central Portugal, not too far from my house. I had great fun driving around the mountains and the Aldeias do Xisto (my house has the same architectural style so characteristic of this region) and getting to know Central Portugal while living in a youth hostel, where I also made my first Portuguese friends.

After a few more legal hiccups (including the owner wanting to keep the keys for the property after I had paid for it), the house was finally mine. I spent a month cleaning, painting and killing fleas and then I moved in.

The neighbours in my tiny, isolated village were overwhelmingly friendly and even persuaded me to adopt one of their puppies. I also had my cat from Australia shipped over, at great expense and hassle, but now we were a happy furry family. Despite everything we had been through, the old house still had the magic for me, and even today I look out of the window at the vista of olives trees and grapevines and sigh.

Hiding away in a remote village in Central Portugal did not stop the global financial crisis from visiting. It didn't happen overnight, but between the share markets plummeting and a huge swing in the Aussie dollar, I lost about half of my remaining money. It had been hard enough finding a builder who shared my vision, but now paying one to *build* my vision was almost impossible. So, much like every expat around here, I put the brakes on spending and sat tight for a while. Instead of building I started writing, and while it hasn't solved my financial dilemma, it has given my life a new, creative angle.

Meanwhile almost all of my vast Australian family and many Aussie friends came to see the house. Be warned, house-hunters: you can't keep the visitors away! Some were a bit shocked by my radical change of lifestyle, but many fell in love with the place. "It's so quiet!" "So unstressful!" "There's no TV!"

Today the house still isn't built, but what's the rush? I'm still cooking over the fireplace and carrying water in and out of the house, but the pets and I have a roof over our heads and we don't go hungry. I wouldn't go back to working 15-hour days and getting stuck in traffic for all the dishwashers in the world.

Emma Brunton,
near Lousã, Central Portugal
www.emmashouseinportugal.com

Real Estate Agents and Vendors

On deciding to buy a property in Portugal most people head straight for the local agents in the area that they are looking in or, if back in the UK, surf around the Internet to see what they can find. There is nothing wrong with either approach. However, do you really know who is doing the selling and whether they should be or not?

Whether you decide to buy a new-build on a development, a resale property, a plot to build on or a countryside ruin, you should make sure of the reputation and credentials of those you are dealing with.

While there are those with a first class reputation, and professionalism and integrity in their dealings, there are of course others, who unfortunately have no conscience or scruples, and who would sell you their grandmother if they could!

So, how can you really know? How can you find out about who you are dealing with?

While nothing is ever 100% certain in the property world, there are some checks you can make to safeguard yourself.

Checking Out Portuguese Agents

In Portugal, a real estate agent has to be registered and, therefore, have the appropriate insurance and professional qualifications. A registered agent is given a number. This is known as an *AMI Nº* and is issued by *INCI (Instituto da Construção e do Imobiliário)*, who are the regulatory body for all estate agents in Portugal.

To check whether a real estate agent is registered and has an *AMI Nº*, consult the *INCI* website at *www.inci.pt*.

Click on *Mediação* on the left-hand side, followed by *Consulta*.

You can then insert all or any of the following: *AMI Nº (Nº Licença)*, company fiscal Nº *(NIPC)*, name *(Denominação)*, address *(Morada)*, postal code *(Código Postal)* or locality *(Localidade)* and click on *Pesquisar* in the bottom right-hand corner.

If you want to find all the registered real estate agents in a particular district *(Distrito)* or council area *(Concelho)* click on the arrows alongside the relevant boxes, highlight the area you want and then click on *Pesquisar*. By clicking on an individual agent you can check all their details, such as when their licence was issued *(Licença emitida em)*, when their licence is valid to *(Válida até)*, their company fiscal Nº *(NIPC)*, their insurance company *(Seguradora)* and the validity date of their insurance *(Data de Validade do Seguro)*.

It has been known for real estate agents to display a false *AMI Nº*. So, just because they *seem* to be legitimate, don't take it for granted — double check.

The *AMI Nº* should be displayed on their website (as well as the title *mediação imobiliária*) and on all company documentation. Agents should also carry an ID card issued by *INCI*.

Some real estate agents may also be members of *APEMIP*. This is an association for real estate agents in Portugal. The website can be viewed in both Portuguese and English at *www.apemip.pt*.

A real estate agent must be in possession of copies of all paperwork and documents relating to the property for sale. Information on these documents can be found in the *What's What* chapter.

Treat all real estate agents the same way. Just because they might be a fellow national and/or speak your language fluently, it doesn't make them any more reputable or trustworthy. Check them out.

More recently, if a real estate agent is involved in the sale of a property, then their name and details must also appear on the final deed *(escritura)*. If you wish to check whether the real estate agent is a limited *(lda)* company and the details of that company, read the *Builders & Architects* chapter to find out how you can do this via the Internet on the *Portal da Empresa* website.

If you need to contact *INCI* to make further enquiries or to make a complaint click on *Contactos* on the home page in the top under the banner or on *Contacte-Nos* at the very top on the left-hand side.

Anyone offering a service to the public also needs a complaints book (*livro de reclamações*) and a real estate agent is no exception. You are entitled to request and complete this book (usually a pad in triplicate) at any time. Any entity being complained about has five working days in which to submit this complaint to the relevant competent authority.

Complaints can then be followed up online at *http://rtic.consumidor.pt* by clicking on *01 Consumidores e Operadores Económicos* and putting in your passport and complaint number, which should be on your copy of the complaint form.

Remember, in Portugal, legal representatives are not permitted to act as real estate agents and sell properties.

Checking Out UK Agents

There are several UK companies on the Internet now selling property and plots in Portugal. They are sometimes connected to a builder or developer and these, of course, will not be registered by *INCI*. Therefore, you should remember that you will not be protected by Portuguese Law should anything go wrong.

Many of these companies are simply run from homes or behind other businesses and when you telephone or email them they will often put you in contact with someone in Portugal. Do your homework again. Check whether they are registered at Companies House in the UK.

Go to *www.companieshouse.gov.uk* and click on *Go to our WebCheck service to search company names and details, order documents and reports*. Enter the name of the company and click on *Search*.

A list will appear with companies of that name or similar. Click on the number of the company you are looking for and if they are registered correctly the company details, such as the registered office address, company number, date of incorporation, company type, nature of business, status, and accounting and return dates will be shown.

To find out more details, such as the directors' names and for copies of returns and accounts, you can click on 'Order information on this company' on the right-hand side, or telephone, write to or email Companies House. They charge a fee for this service.

Check also when you contact the real estate company in the UK, whether they have an office in Portugal and, therefore, the address, telephone and fax numbers, mobile numbers and email address for that office, as well as the name of the contact in Portugal.

There are also UK based companies with Portuguese real estate 'arms' doing viewing trips for a very cheap fee per person. However, a long weekend is rarely enough time to view enough properties sufficiently. Secondly, they aren't giving you a good price on the viewing trip simply because they're nice. Their goal is to sell you property. So, if you do decide to go on one of these trips be prepared for their pressure selling tricks and don't let anyone rush you to make a decision.

Consider these companies in the same light as you would any other and make sure you do the necessary checks.

Checking Out Private Vendors

Of course there are people who prefer to sell privately. No problem in that. But check that the person selling the property actually owns it. It may sound bizarre, but there have been cases of people buying houses from individuals, who don't actually own them! Not very nice when the real owners come back to claim them.

Also, check how many people own the property. Quite often the title can be in the name of several family members and if one of them happens to be living overseas, it can be very difficult getting them all to agree to sell and sign. See the *Land Registry — Conservatória do Registo Predial* and *Notary — Cartório Notarial* sections of the *What's What* chapter to find out how you can check, regarding who the owners of a property are.

Other Checks You Should Carry Out

Check that the property you are buying is actually destined for habitation and not a garage, warehouse or any other type of building. It should have a habitation licence or pre-1951 certificate, and, on the previous deeds, *caderneta* and land registry certificates, it should state *Casa de Habitação* and not any of the following as its main usage: garage (*garagem*), warehouse (*armazem*), storage building (*arrumos*), commercial use (*comercial*) or oil press (*lagar*). See the *What's What* chapter for more information on all these documents.

If you are buying a plot of land, in order to have a house built, then check that you can actually build on it. Even if there is already a ruin on the plot, don't just assume you can go ahead and build. Planning rules regularly change and land you cannot build on is of little value. Don't just take verbal confirmation from agents and others.

Check what type of land you are buying, that is, how it is classified. Is it urban and designated for construction? Or is it rustic, agricultural and/or ecological?

How is the land zoned? What size property can you build on it, or by how much can you extend what is already there?

Go to the local council *(câmara municipal)* to ask these questions and find out whether you will get approval for your intended project or works. Get anything they say confirmed in writing by asking for a viability of construction *(informação/comunicação prévia — viabilidade de construção).*

Check with your individual local council as to the period of validity of this document. In the past it took approximately one month to obtain and could last up to a year, but as things often change in Portugal make sure you confirm this and perhaps enlist the help of a local architect.

You can also ask to see the *PDM (Plano Desenvolvimento Municipal).* This is the municipal development plan and is renewed every 10 years. It states what can be built in different areas. Ask when it is due for renewal and if it is near its end, ask if they have a renewal one ready. Some local councils have this information online.

You can find your local council at http://www.cm-(your_town).pt, for example Faro council would be *www.cm-faro.pt. PDM* information can also be obtained from the Directorate General for Urban Development and Territorial Planning (*Direcção-Geral do Ordenamento do Território e Desenvolvimento Urbano – DGOTDU*) at *www.dgotdu.pt.*

Remember that while, in a country like the UK, planning permission can take up to six weeks, in Portugal it could take anything up to a year! See the *Builders & Architects'* chapter for more on this.

In Portugal when the property for sale is either rustic (*prédio rústico*) or mixed, i.e. rustic and urban (*prédio misto*), the adjoining neighbours will have first refusal on it. This is called *Exercício de Direito de Preferência.* If you put in an offer for a property and the price and date for completion are agreed, then you should check that the neighbours have been notified and get it in writing from them that they have no interest in purchasing it.

The real estate agent should have done this for you, but double check. If not, they could have the right to claim the property at the agreed price several years down the line!

Check where the boundaries to the property are exactly situated. Get a map from the local council or from the Portuguese Geography Institute *(Instituto Geográfico Português – IGEO* – more on that in the *Maps* section of the *What's What* chapter) and walk the land with the owner, noting where the markers are. In the countryside the boundaries are usually denoted with large stone markers splashed with white paint.

IGEO maps are not always as accurate as you might hope though, so if there are any doubts, ask for a surveyor to carry out a topographical survey and mark out the boundaries.

Check if there are any public rights of way that cross the property and if you wish to add a track or access road, that you will get permission from the local council to do so. If the track/road is going to cross anyone else's land, you will also need to seek their written permission. Make sure that you have complete and legal access to the property you wish to purchase.

Remember, a nice view can disappear instantly if somebody builds on it. If there is any land for sale in front of the property you are interested in purchasing, then you cannot guarantee that it will stay the way it is now forever.

Check that everything in the property works, for example: boilers, electricity, fitted appliances, heating systems and swimming pool equipment. Don't just take the vendor's and real estate agent's word for it. If the property has been built within the last five years, then ask to see the builder's guarantee. These are usually transferable to the new owner.

Also ask what will remain in the property as part of the sale. Some Portuguese owners will even take the kitchen sink with them, as well as all the light fittings and bulbs; so don't just make an assumption.

It is quite rare for foreign purchasers in Portugal to request property surveys if they are not requiring any form of bank loan and even then the banks tend to send an architect or engineer, as opposed to a trained surveyor. However, it is well worth considering getting a survey done, especially for older properties.

Remember to deal with buying a property in Portugal in exactly the same way as you would back home. Make sure if you are going to use a fellow national as the surveyor that they are knowledgeable in Portuguese construction methods and ask them if they have professional indemnity insurance. Ask them what will be included and what won't be included in the report.

Another option, which might be more cost effective, would be to ask a reputable builder to take a look at the property, as they will be able to give you an idea of the cost to repair or renovate any potential problems, something a surveyor may not be able to do.

Check what plans there are for the immediate area at the local council, in terms of developments, roads, shops, etc, which may be to your advantage, or conversely, have an adverse effect on the property. Check the *PDM* mentioned above to also see what type of land you are surrounded by and the likely level of building to take place in the future.

If you wish to add a swimming pool to the property, or check about the legalities of an existing one, then see the *Swimming Pool Licences* section of the *What's What* chapter.

Other checks you should carry out can be found in the following chapters. A property purchase checklist can also be found at the back of the book.

NATIVE'S TIP

If you receive any objections or obstructions from the vendor or real estate agent in relation to any of the checks you wish to carry out then ask yourself what they may be hiding and whether you still want to go ahead with the purchase. There are plenty of properties out there. Think carefully!

CASE STUDY: SOPHIE & ANDY

We have lived in Central Portugal for seven years, bringing up our three children, running our own business, and creating and looking after a smallholding. We came here from Brighton, UK where we had been running a business helping people set up worker and housing co-operatives (Andy), co-ordinating a Friends of the Earth group (Sophie), home-schooling our children, and growing a few vegetables in the backyard. We arrived in Portugal as part of a camper van tour of Europe, and never went home again! We spent a year living in the van on a *quinta* (smallholding) in return for our help on the land, while searching for a property to buy, and another year living in a yurt (Mongolian tent) while renovating a ruin.

We hope we can offer you some tips and advice, based on our experience, for your own move to Portugal, and how to ensure it doesn't cost the earth.

Choosing a Property

Try to put UK prices out of your mind! Also try not to sweat over whether you are getting a bargain or being ripped off (though if you follow the advice in this book, the latter shouldn't happen!). A property is worth whatever you are happy to pay for it — after all, this is going to be your home, your new life, and your dream! We're not suggesting you spend recklessly, but just don't get too hung up on other people's ideas of a property's (monetary) value.

Think carefully about what you want now, and what you might want/need in the future. Will you want to grow vegetables? Then your own water source (well, spring, or 'water mine') is going to be essential as water is metered in Portugal. How hot do you like it? Portuguese summers are hot and dry and, although this might sound like paradise, you'll soon be searching out some shade — so beware the property adverts that state 'good sun exposure'! How much land do you need? Due to the risk of forest fires in Portugal, you are required by law to keep your land clear, so more land equals more work (though I could write another article just on how to reduce this work and the risk of fire!).

Be prepared to compromise, but write a carefully considered list of your must-haves to help keep you focused. We had 'own plentiful water supply' on our must-have list, and 'waterfall, stream, or sound of running water' on our 'would be nice to have' list. Think about what you are prepared to create yourself if it's on your must-have list but missing from the property — for example, must have a garage, or the possibility to *build* one.

Setting Yourselves Up

To help spread the cost of the tools we knew we'd need once we had some land, we budgeted to buy one tool a week from the local market. (When I saw a machete I wanted, but that was too big and heavy for me, the stallholder handed me a piece of chalk to draw the size I wanted on the blade and told me to come back next week and he would have cut it down for me — which he did, for no extra charge). Start now to build up a supply of anything you don't already have, that you think you'll need. Don't scrimp; buy quality that will last a lifetime. Tip: you can't get English-style digging forks in Portugal — bring them with you!

The same principle applies to other equipment and furnishings (washing machine, wardrobe, donkey cart): buy things on special offer now, if you know you'll need them in six months.

Reducing Spending and Monthly Bills

Spend money now on setting yourselves up so you'll need very little for everyday expenses — *invest in the future!* Install solar electricity and water heating, build or renovate a thermally efficient house (make use of the sun's orientation and get the best insulation you can afford), and don't scrimp on efficient heating (better to pay now for the best stove than later in fuel) — and make sure that fuel is from a renewable source as fossil fuel prices are set to rocket over the next few years.

Abide by the permaculture principle 'waste is just an unused resource' and try to ensure that everything has more than one use — a goat will give milk *and* keep your brambles under control; chickens turn your kitchen scraps into eggs and manure; and a compost heap is your kitchen waste disposal *and* next year's fertile soil for pot plants.

Making a Living

Use the skills you have and think outside the box. You might not get the same type of job you have now, but you can almost certainly use some of the skills you've picked up along the way, and you should find you can also put your interests to good use. We put together our personal interest in property (particularly rural property and renovation projects) with our web design and marketing skills and created Pure Portugal Ltd. (an online business advertising properties for sale and holiday accommodation in the region). In addition to trying to use your existing skills, be prepared to turn your hand to anything! In the early days we mostly cleared other people's brambles!

A word on holiday rentals: you are not the first to come to this beautiful part of Portugal, see its tourism potential, and decide *this* is how you are going to make your living. The market has become saturated. By all means offer holiday rentals to supplement your income (we have three yurts we rent out), but don't bank on it covering your necessary expenses.

Making the Move

For us, I think a willingness to go with the flow and accept what life gives (and sometimes throws at) us has been invaluable. Too often you can find yourself stuck with a job, mortgage, school or bills wanting a way out, but unable to see how this might be possible.

We would therefore heartily recommend that you follow your dreams, don't worry too much about the practical stuff, and just *go for it*!

Maybe my advice should come with a health warning, because we're telling you to throw caution to the wind, follow your dreams, and act like you've nothing to lose! What's important to you? The latest big-screen, high-definition TV with a gazillion channels? Well, in that case, I'd advise you to stay home watching it. But if *real* quality of life is what you're after, then make the move! No, it probably won't be easy, but we guarantee you it'll be worth it.

Sophie & Andy, Central Portugal

www.pureportugal.co.uk

www.pureportugalholidays.com

www.portugalsmallholding.org

www.portugalyurt.co.uk

Builders and Architects

If you decide to buy directly from a builder or developer, have them build a new house on a plot, or have any work done on the property you are purchasing, such as renovations or extensions, then make some checks. The same applies to using an architect.

Checking Out Your Builder

A builder, who undertakes large renovation works or projects, as opposed to minor repairs, must be a registered builder and should have a building permit *(Alvará de Construção)*. These are renewed annually and can be checked on the *INCI* website.

To check for builders' permits go to *www.inci.pt* and click on *Construção* on the left-hand side followed by *Consulta de Empresas* and then *Alvará.*

You can then insert all or any of the following: building permit N° *(Alvará)*, individual or company fiscal N° *(NIF/NIPC)*, company/builder's name *(Denominação)*, postal code *(Código Postal)* or locality *(Localidade)*, before clicking on *Pesquisar* in the bottom right-hand corner.

If you want to find all registered builders in a particular district *(Distrito)* or council area *(Concelho)*, click on the arrows alongside the relevant boxes and highlight the area you want and then click on *Pesquisar*. By clicking on the individual builder you can then check all their details, such as the validity date of the building permit *(Data de Validade)*, their individual or company fiscal Nº *(NIF/NIPC)*, their address *(Morada)*, when they first registered *(Data de Inscrição)* and the categories *(Categorias/Habilitações)* — i.e. the type and size of works they can carry out. The licence depends on such things, as the type of equipment they have and the number of qualified staff the company has on board.

Builders undertaking more minor works should have a *Título de Registo*. These are valid for five years and then renewed. A builder working under a *Título de Registo* has a limit of €16.600 for his works at the time of writing in 2011.

To check if a builder has a *Título de Registo* go to *www.inci.pt* and click on *Construção* on the left-hand side followed by *Consulta de Empresas* and then *Título de Registo*.

Follow the same steps as for searching for a builder's permit *(Alvará)* above. There are many more categories for builders with a *Título de Registo* and you might need some help deciphering them.

If you need to contact *INCI* to make further enquiries or to make a complaint click on *Contactos* on the home page in the top under the banner or on *Contacte-Nos* at the very top on the left-hand side.

Remember the complaints book (*livro de reclamações*) mentioned in the *Real Estate Agents & Vendors'* chapter can also be requested for complaints.

If you want to find out if your builder is a limited company, you can check by consulting the *Portal da Empresa* website at *www.portaldaempresa.pt*.

Click on *empresa online* at the top of the page followed by *Pesquisa de nomes (firmas ou denominações) existentes* under *Pedido de nome* halfway down on the left-hand side. Enter the name of the company that you wish to find where it says *Nome,* and then click on *Pesquisar*. You can also add in the council area (*Concelho*), if you wish to narrow down your search.

If after trying this you still do not find the company you are looking for, you can contact the local commercial registry office *(conservatória do registo comercial)* in the area where the company is situated to double check. At this office, you can also obtain more information on a company, for example directors' names and formation date, etc. You may have to pay a few Euros to obtain this information. To find the address of your local office, go to *www.irn.mj.pt/IRN/sections/irn/contactos* and click on *Conservatórias de registo commercial* under the *serviços desconcentrados do IRN, I.P.* subheading. You can then download the file. This will give you a list of all the *conservatórias do registo commercial* in Portugal.

Note that electricians and gas fitters in Portugal must also be registered and licensed. Your builder will usually recommend these technicians to you. Utility companies will not certify an installation and make a connection unless it has been fitted by a qualified, registered technician.

Checking Out Your Architect

To make checks on an architect, in order to see that they are correctly registered, go to the *Ordem dos Arquitectos* website at *www.arquitectos.pt* and click on *para o público* at the top followed by *consulte um arquitecto* on the left-hand side and *encontre um arquitecto* on the right.

Insert the name of the architect in the box marked *Nome* and then click on *Pesquisar*. If you need to contact the *Ordem dos Arquitectos* to make any further enquiries or a complaint, go to the top right-hand side of the home page and click on *Contactos*.

Note that there are many people in Portugal working as if they are architects when they are, in fact, only a draftsman/woman regulated by the local council *(câmara municipal)*. They need to have their work signed off by a fully qualified architect. Make sure that you know exactly what you are getting for your money. If you want a qualified, graduate architect, then check that they are with their governing body, as detailed above.

You may also need the services of an engineer during the planning and construction stages. The architect will quite often work alongside an engineer, but if you wish to find one yourself or check that they are registered with their professional body, then you can make enquiries with the *Ordem dos Engenheiros* at *www.ordemengenheiros.pt*. At the time of writing it was not possible to consult an online directory, but to contact this body click on *Contactos* at the very bottom and then on the region (*região*).

As of 2008, an engineer must sign off a project, as well as the architect.

Planning Procedure

As mentioned in the *Real Estate Agents & Vendors'* chapter, planning permission in Portugal can take a very long time (from six months to a year), so you should be prepared for a long wait and not try to rush things. It is also never advisable to start any building works without the correct permissions and licences.

Planning permission in Portugal has tightened up considerably over the last few years and as well as facing the possibility of large fines from the local council, you could also now be left with an illegal property, which may be difficult to sell at a later date.

Minor works, maintenance, restoration and repairs that do not alter the façade of a property, as well as internal works that do not alter the structure of a property generally do not need planning permission. However, it is always best to check with the local council (*câmara municipal*) first.

The architect will prepare all the documentation and plans to request a construction licence. He or she should also supervise the work that the builder carries out to make sure that it is completed according to the plans and to the necessary standard, and must sign off the book of works (*Livro de Obra*).

The first stage of planning is called the Architectural Project (*Projecto de Arquitectura*). It is a comprehensive brief including architectural drawings, a topographical survey and a list of the materials to be used. This is submitted to the local council first for approval.

The second stage is called the Specialities Project (*Projecto de Especialidades*). This part of the project covers the engineering required to complete the build, e.g. information on septic waste removal, water, etc. and is usually compiled in conjunction with an engineer.

Once both the *Projecto de Arquitectura* and *Projecto de Especialidades* have been approved, your chosen builder (with his building permit and proof of insurance cover) can then obtain the building licence (*alvará de construção*) from the local council. They will also issue the builder with a notice (*aviso*) to be displayed outside the construction site showing that they have permission to build.

When the property has been completed, the builder must arrange for an inspection (*vistória*) by the local council. This request must also be accompanied by a declaration from the supervising architect or engineer that the building has been constructed according to the plans and building regulations. This person should be someone registered with the local council with legal permission to make such declarations.

Note that the local council can also make inspections at any point during the works, if they so choose.

Recent changes to the regulations in March 2008 have meant that a local council inspection may not always be required, unless the architect or engineer does not take full responsibility for the works.

A habitation licence *(licença de habitação)* will then be issued if all is correct.

The final payment to your builder should not be made until you have received the habitation licence.

As of March 30th 2004 a builder now also needs to produce a *ficha técnica de habitação* (*FTH*). See the *Habitation Licence, Pre-1951 Certificate and Ficha Técnica de Habitação* section of the *What's What* chapter.

The property must then be registered at the local tax office *(serviço das finanças)* and land registry *(conservatória do registo predial)*.

The builder should also supply you with a five-year warranty against any structural defects. Make sure that you get this warranty in writing. However, remember that this does not exclude you from getting your own structural property insurance.

Recommendations

When seeking an architect or builder, get independent recommendations and references from other people and go to see some of their previous work. A local builder may also be preferable to one from a different part of the country.

There are plenty of forums on the Internet now for Portugal, so this can be another means of swapping information and recommendations. The same method could be used for real estate agents and legal representatives.

Be aware that a real estate agent might be on commission from a builder and/or architect, so they aren't necessarily the best people to ask to make a recommendation. It is also a good idea to use an architect who is independent from the builder.

Translation and Supervision

Make sure you are precise about everything you want done and include everything. Don't be vague and don't make assumptions. If there are any doubts due to language difficulties then use an independent translator.

If you are not going to be around to supervise the work then you may need to consider having someone do this on your behalf, or to employ a project manager. As with everything else involved in buying a property in

Portugal, don't cut corners and try to save a little bit on the expense. You may find that it will land you in deeper financial problems further down the line.

It is a good idea to get a Portuguese-speaking friend or Portuguese translator to go with you to check each stage at the local council *(câmara municipal)*. You can inspect any planning file, although sometimes you have to request the file a day in advance, which enables you to make sure that what your builder/architect is telling you is true and that you are not being fobbed off.

Buying From a Builder and Building Contracts

Buying a plot of land from a builder and then having him also do the work is not always a good idea. Compare the prices of similar plots in the area, as well as the building costs with other builders.

If you do decide to go ahead with the same builder then make sure that you have two contracts drawn up, one for the land and one for the building, and get the land deed title sorted out first before doing the building contract.

Check also that the builder actually owns the land he is selling and if not, who does? It is obviously the owner's name that must appear on the deed *(escritura)*.

Buying off plan is still a popular means of buying a property in Portugal but it can have its drawbacks. If a builder goes bankrupt then your property could remain unfinished, or while your property might have been completed, it could end up sitting on an unfinished development.

It is wise to check if your builder has an insurance policy, which will protect you in the event that the company goes bust. It isn't unusual to be asked for an amount of money to act as a small holding deposit, in order to reserve a property before the promissory contract *(contrato de promessa de compra e venda)* is signed. Obviously this should be well documented and invoiced.

For buying off plan or employing a builder to build a property on a plot, you should seek the advice of a legal representative in the drawing up of a contract.

The contract should include:

- ❑ The stage payments (which can vary in percentages).
- ❑ Dates for the stage payments.
- ❑ A timetable for completion to tie up with the payments.
- ❑ A date for completion.
- ❑ Penalties for failure to complete on time.
- ❑ Guarantees.
- ❑ Insurance policy against non-completion.
- ❑ A copy of the plans and drawings and any clauses.
- ❑ An amount for a set period of time to act as a guarantee against the builder not addressing any faults.

Make sure that the work to be done at each stage is complete before parting with money, as the percentage of construction work carried out is more important than just dates and times. Do not give any more money than the contract states at each stage.

In relation to buying off plan you must also consider that, unlike the UK, there is no leasehold system. Apartments, and occasionally townhouses and some semi-detached properties, are sold under a system of horizontal property *(propriedade horizontal)*. A builder must sign a deed at the notary *(cartório notarial)* in order to create this system and, therefore, set up individual legal titles for each unit. These individual titles are then registered at the land registry *(conservatória do registo predial)* and each is given an individual title number.

The deed of horizontal property should include:

- ❑ The relative value of each unit in the form of a percentage of the whole building.
- ❑ The authorised use of each unit.
- ❑ The condominium rules and restrictions – including details of the administration and maintenance.
- ❑ What makes up the communal parts.
- ❑ Arbitration rules in the event of any disputes between owners.

Also see the *Condominiums* chapter.

Paying Builders and Architects

When using a builder or architect for any work, regardless of whether it is a small job or not, ask for invoices *(facturas)* for everything. Pay the VAT *(IVA* – currently 21%). It may seem 'like getting blood out of a stone' at times — but don't take no for an answer. These invoices may help to reduce your capital gains tax liability if you later want to sell the property. They are valid for five years from the date of purchase for this reason, and so saving a bit of tax here and there now could cost you dearly later.

You might also need proof that they did the work if you ever need to call them back at a later stage because of defective workmanship. Do not pay 'cash in hand' for anything.

Discuss with your bank and/or financial adviser the best way to make any payments to your builder or architect so that your money can be accounted for.

Builders and Legal Advice

It is a bad idea to use a lawyer *(advogado)* or *solicitador(a)* recommended by a builder, or in any way associated to a builder/development company. This can be a recipe for disaster due to vested interests. If you use their legal representative then how will you know if they are acting in *your* best interests and not those of the builder/developer when they draw up the contract? See the chapter on *Professional Legal Advice*.

CASE STUDY: HAZEL GILL

I am originally from Edinburgh and my partner and I moved to Portugal in February 2008. I have been coming to Central Portugal for seven years, since my mum moved here. She buys and sells properties and we had invested in a property together back in 2004. After selling our first property for a profit, we then purchased another in a little village, which both my partner and I fell in love with. It was a ruin and needed a lot of renovating, but as mum had worked for a long time with the same builder, renovating many other properties, it wasn't too scary! When we moved over in February, we were hoping to move straight into our new home, but of course, these things take time. Some people can't seem to understand this, coming from the UK where people are always rushing to complain if things aren't done on time!

A lot of people also couldn't understand why my partner and I moved to such a rural part of Portugal after living in the city, as we are very young to be taking such a leap. I am 28 and my partner is 29. Basically, we were looking to get onto the property market in Edinburgh, which proved very difficult, and we were also in stressful jobs, which we hated. I was manager of a clothes shop on Princes Street and my partner worked for a bank. So we decided that, as we were young, it was worth the risk and if things didn't work, we could always go back. Saying that, we are still here after two and a half years. It is quiet here, but that's how we like it. Back in the UK, the weekend would come and we'd go out at 10pm and have a few drinks with mates, but here it is much more of a café culture and, as it is so cheap to eat out in most places, people go out for lunches and drinks during the day.

We didn't have a clear-cut plan for work when we moved to Portugal, but took the attitude that we would try our hand at anything. My partner has gone from banker to construction, landscape gardener, general maintenance, and anything guy! I clean rental accommodations and I have also set up an online business selling corsets and corset dresses. I studied corset-making at university and worked for Vivienne Westwood in London, so it is great now to be finally doing what I enjoy. When I am not cleaning, I am working away in my sweatshop making things to put on the Internet for order. It is lovely to take a break for lunch and sit on the terrace in the beautiful sunshine (which makes all the difference) looking out onto the forest. It's also nice not to get that sick feeling I used to have in my stomach on a Sunday night when I knew I had to work the next day.

While our house was being renovated, we had a stray dog in the garden, and my mum and I would bring scraps for him when we came to check on the progress of the house. My partner kept saying that we weren't keeping the dog, but as I am typing he is stroking its belly. It is not pleasant to see all the strays about, but I'm very happy that we could help one and maybe in the future we can help some more. There are so many to be helped that I can't quite understand people who come over with dogs they have paid a lot of money for and that are not used to the climate! You do have to train yourself to harden your heart when it comes to the treatment of animals here. Unfortunately there is no RSPCA equivalent here and even if there were, I don't know where they would start.

Since moving here, I have discovered a love of gardening, as things grow so easily. My partner has a vegetable patch, which I am not allowed to touch! The vegetables taste so much better when they are home grown. The food is also much healthier. In the summertime we live on salads, and in the winter, lots of vegetable soup. You can recreate most English meals with local ingredients and, when you can't, it doesn't matter as you can try the Portuguese food and new recipes. We also have a large bread oven in our courtyard, which my partner cooked Christmas dinner in last year. We also have about 50 vines, and last year my mum's partner added some to their crop so they could make homemade wine. I think this year we might try making some ourselves; I quite like the idea of trampling grapes with my feet although I don't know how many people will want to drink it after!

The cost of living here is very low. On a monthly basis we spend about a third of what we spent in the UK. Food and wine is cheap, though some things do cost more here, like cars and electrical equipment. The Portuguese people are lovely. Our neighbours are always giving us fruit from their fruit trees, jams, flowers and so on. The language does take time to learn and you find some people are easier to understand than others, but on the whole people are very accommodating and patient when you are speaking with them. Of course, the more you practise when out and about, the better you become. I always say that my partner's Portuguese improves considerably after a few bottles of Sagres!

It has been difficult at times not having a regular income, and we miss our family and friends. But we have no regrets and absolutely love it here – and our loved ones know where to visit for a holiday.

Hazel Gill, Central Portugal

www.hgfashions.webs.com

http://myworld.ebay.co.uk/hazeljg1982

Professional Legal Advice

Foreigners unable to speak Portuguese, or only a limited degree, often decide to rely on using some form of legal advice when buying property in Portugal.

Types of Representative

You may approach either a *solicitador(a)* or an *advogado(a)* for legal representation.

A *solicitador(a)*, despite the similarity of the name to the English solicitor, is not the same. In Portugal, a *solicitador(a)* is more akin to someone who does conveyancing, or a legal executive. They do not have to study for a degree and are not permitted to do court work. They are regulated by the *Câmara dos Solicitadores*.

You can **check whether a *solicitador(a)* is registered with the *Câmara dos Solicitadores*** by going to *www.solicitador.net*.

Go to *Pesquisa Solicitador* at the bottom of the left-hand column and put in whatever information you have about the *solicitador(a)* you are searching for, such as: surname *(Apelido)*, first name *(Nome)*, town/area *(Comarca)*, postal code *(Código Postal*), registered number (*Cédula*) and then click on *Pesquisar*.

A list of *solicitadores* with that surname in that area should then appear, each with their address (*Morada*) and registered numbers *(Cédula Nºs)*.

To check for firms of *solicitadores,* click on *Pesquisar sociedades* underneath the individual search boxes and put in the name *(Nome)* and/or the area/town *(Localidade)* and then click on *Pesquisar*.

An *advogado(a)*, is the equivalent of a lawyer, barrister or solicitor in the UK. Not all *advogado(a)s* specialise, so you could find a lawyer dealing with a property purchase one day, a divorce the day after that and in court defending a criminal the day after that. However, if you want to find a specialist property lawyer, it may well be worth the extra expense.

Lawyers study for five years at university and gain the title *Dr(a)* if they graduate. They are regulated by the *Ordem dos Advogados*.

To **check that an *advogado(a)* is qualified**, and what their principal practising address and registered Nº *(cédula Nº)* is, go to *www.oa.pt* and click on *Pesquisa de advogados* on the left-hand side.

Put the lawyer's name in the box marked *Nome* and click on *Procurar* or the magnifying glass symbol. Their address, telephone/fax numbers, email address and registered Nº should all be listed. If a number of lawyers come up with the same or similar names, then you can narrow down your search by putting in their office address (*Morada*), postcode (*Código Postal*), or town (*Comarca*). You can also search by council district (*Conselho Distrital*) or registered number (*Cédula*), if known. You can list in order of the above categories by clicking on *Ordenar Por*.

Surprisingly, *advogado(a)s* are not obliged to register all their practising addresses, but only a principal office. Lawyers have been found to have one address listed with the *Ordem dos Advogados* and a completely different one in the yellow pages *(páginas amarelas)*. The Portuguese yellow pages can be found in both Portuguese and English at *www.pai.pt*.

Many lawyers work together as a firm and you should check on this when employing an individual lawyer.

The *Ordem dos Advogados* website is currently not listing details of firms, but should you wish to check on this then you can contact them by telephone. They usually have an English speaking operative on their switchboard, if required. Click on *Contactos* in the top right-hand corner on the home page for their contact details.

Doing Your Own Checks

In an ideal world using a legal representative should mean that you are protected and that you receive honest and good advice. However, just because someone has a degree, a title and a few initials after their name, it does not guarantee that they will behave in a moral and ethical manner.

It is strongly recommended that you also do your own checks alongside those of your legal representative. This way you can cross-reference with your legal representative and get clarification for anything that you are not sure about. If you don't speak Portuguese yourself, take an independent Portuguese translator, or reliable Portuguese-speaking friend, to do these checks. Don't cut corners on this because of the extra time or expense. It could cost you considerably more later.

Selecting Your Legal Representative

Many real estate agents, builders and developers will recommend a lawyer or *solicitador(a)* to you. This will more often than not be *their* lawyer or *solicitador(a)*.

It is much better to choose your own independent legal representation. If you don't, you can never be sure that they will be acting in your best interests and not those of the vendor. Get recommendations from other people whenever possible.

It has also been known for a lawyer to act for both vendor and purchaser. This is not permitted and totally unethical. Another practice is to sometimes get a lawyer 'friend' (often working from the same office) to deal with the other party. In effect, the purchase and sale is then still very much 'under one roof'.

Use your common sense when selecting your legal advice and keep a close eye on proceedings. Ask for quotations from a few lawyers/*solicitadores*. On average they charge 1 to 1.5% of the property purchase value for their legal fees. However, this can be quite variable depending on the area in Portugal and it has been known for some to charge as much as 2.5% and others as little as 0.5%. Remember that going for the cheapest lawyer, in order to try to save money isn't necessarily the best idea.

What You Should Expect

Make sure that they set down exactly what they will be doing via an engagement letter, which should confirm the terms and conditions of how they will be acting on your behalf. Find out, for example, if they are going to be dealing with the change over of contracts for the various utility services as well as the property searches.

Don't proceed without an engagement letter. Make sure that you get every step clarified in writing from your legal representative. Try to insist on receiving hard copies on their official headed stationery. Don't just accept faxes or emails for other than routine matters.

Check with the *Ordem dos Advogados* if a lawyer is an individual or an associate in a firm of lawyers, as detailed above, and is, therefore, using the right headed stationery.

You should also insist on an invoice *(factura)* for any money you pay to your legal representative on proper-headed stationery, which should also show their fiscal number (*número de contribuinte* or *NIF*), together with a 'narrative' itemising everything that they have done on your behalf.

Remember, that as well as the legal fees, you will also have to pay:

- Notary fees.
- Deed (*escritura*) registration fees.
- Stamp duty (0.8%).
- Purchase tax (*imposto municipal sobre transmissões onerosas de imóveis — IMT*).

See the Appendix for 2011 *IMT* rates.

Figures of 10 to 15% of the purchase price have often been quoted for the above fees, but more recent research has shown that figures of 3 to 5% to be perhaps more realistic. However, always get a detailed breakdown of these costs for your individual circumstances, so that there are no unexpected expenses. Speak to your legal representative and a financial adviser about this.

Remember, it is also not permitted for your legal representative to make money on your money in his/her client account. So make sure that you get a firm date at the notary to sign the final deed and transfer the money to coincide with this date.

Why let your money sit in someone else's account while waiting for a convenient slot at the notary to finalise your purchase, or while you are waiting for your legal representative to complete his/her enquiries?

Another way of paying for your property could be by a form of banker's draft *(cheque visado)* direct from a Portuguese bank account, which you can easily set up. You can then hand this cheque over to the vendors on the day of the final deed signing, without having to put your money through anyone else's account. Check with your bank and/or financial adviser about the best method of payment for you.

Finally, make sure you are legitimate yourself. Don't be sweet talked into trying to evade tax or anything else untoward. You may find that if you have a problem further down the line people could try to blackmail you with this to stop you going to the authorities and you could end up a lot worse off.

Promissory Contract

If you decide to pay a deposit (usually 10%) to hold the property and sign a promissory contract *(contrato de promessa de compra e venda)* then make sure that it is checked over or drawn up by a legal representative. Doing this ensures that any clauses you wish to be included are written into the contract. If you withdraw from the sale then you will lose your deposit. If the vendor withdraws then they will have to pay you double.

It is important that you know exactly what you are agreeing to, so get a translation in English and have both the Portuguese and English versions checked by an independent translator to make sure that they are identical.

Never sign anything without being entirely sure what you are agreeing to. You can go straight to the final deed stage without a promissory contract, but when paying a deposit it is usually advisable to get one.

This contract should include:

- ❑ The names, addresses, civil states, nationalities (if non-Portuguese), birthplaces, ID Nºs (ID card/*bilhete de identidade,* residence card or passport) and fiscal numbers (*números de contribuinte*) of both parties.
- ❑ Details and location of the property.
- ❑ Land registry certificate Nº (*certidão de registo predial/teor Nº*).
- ❑ Tax office document Nºs (*caderneta Nºs*).
- ❑ The amount of deposit paid.
- ❑ The agreed purchase price.
- ❑ The agreed date for the final deed signing.

If buying off plan from a builder, then review the earlier chapter on *Builders & Architects* regarding contracts, deposits and payments.

Power of Attorney

Many people give a lawyer or *solicitador(a)* 'power of attorney' – POA (*procurador/a*). There is nothing wrong with this approach and it usually works out well if you are using someone reputable, but how do you know what will go on if you are not there to see and sign it for yourself?

It is advisable to attend any signings, especially the final deed signing, and if you don't speak Portuguese then you must take a translator as you will be asked by the notary *(notário(a))* if you understand everything taking place. It may be best to use an independent translator even if your legal representative is present and speaks English.

Final Deed

The following should appear on the final deed:

- ❑ The names, addresses, civil states, nationalities (if non-Portuguese), birthplaces, ID N°s (ID card/*bilhete de identidade,* residence card or passport) and fiscal numbers (*números de contribuinte*) for both parties.
- ❑ Power of attorney(s), if applicable, and who translated it, if either or both of the parties do not understand Portuguese.
- ❑ Details and location of the property, including which parish (*freguesia*) and council (*concelho*) it falls under.
- ❑ The land registry certificate N° (*certidão de registo predial/teor N°*).
- ❑ Tax office document N°s (*caderneta N°s*).

- Purchase tax (*IMT*) document Nº and (if it is a 'mixed' property possessing both a rustic and urban *caderneta*) how the values are split between rustic (*rústico*) and urban (*urbano*) land.
- The total price paid for the property.
- If a real estate agent was involved, the details of the agent.

The deed should also state that the following documents were presented, along with their appropriate numbers, as well as the dates on which the copies were issued:

- Habitation licence (*licença de habitação*) or pre-1951 certificate (*pre-1951 certidão*).
- *Ficha técnica de habitação* for post March 30th 2004 properties.
- Land registry certificate (*certidão de registo predial/teor*).
- Tax office document(s) for rustic/urban property (*caderneta(s) urbanas/rústicas*).

If there is a mortgage involved, the contract will be drawn up by the bank and signed at the notary office. Before this stage, your legal representative will provisionally register the mortgage at the land registry (*conservatória do registo predial*), which includes the amount of the mortgage. Details of this should also be included on the deed and an official from the bank should be in attendance to sign.

If it is a company selling the property, then a *certidão de registo commercial* should be provided showing the partners and shareholders, who has what powers, and the business details, address, etc. ID and fiscal Nºs for the owner/partners also need to be provided and a power of attorney for the person signing on behalf of the company.

If at all possible, request a copy of the final deed and an English translation a few days before signing. You can then check it through with a translator and take it with you to crosscheck with what you are signing on the day. You can also check that the correct identities for those involved are detailed.

If, at any time, you are not clear or you are unhappy about what is going on then don't feel embarrassed to halt proceedings to clarify anything you wish. The values on the deed will usually be in text only and not numerals, so as yet another safeguard, find out how the amount is written in Portuguese and write it down to take with you.

With regard to making sure that the correct price for the property you are buying goes on the deed, it is not advisable to agree with the vendor to 'under declare' the property value and pay part of the price in cash 'under the table'.

Not only is this practice strictly illegal but it leaves you liable for a heavy fine if discovered by the tax office.

Paying less purchase tax due to this deception might seem a good idea at the time, but it will almost certainly result in a larger capital gains tax bill, if and when you decide to sell the property.

If you are buying a 'mixed' property, that is, a property with both a rustic and urban *caderneta* (see the *Tax Office – Serviço das Finanças* section of the *What's What* chapter for information regarding *cadernetas*) then check how the price is to be divided up between the rustic part and the urban part.

Buildings obviously have a far greater value than rustic land and in general the ratio is 10% on the land and 90% on the house but get reputable financial advice if you have any doubts in this area. Also note that these days all properties are re-valued by the tax office after a purchase has taken place.

If there are any fixtures and fittings involved in the sale of the property then these should be dealt with separately and are independent of the price of the property.

What You Should Receive

Make sure that your legal representative gives you proper authenticated (with a stamp/seal) copies of all documents, such as:

- ❑ Promissory contract.
- ❑ Final deed.
- ❑ Land registry certificate.
- ❑ Purchase tax (*IMT*) invoice.

- ❑ Habitation licence or pre-1951 certificate.
- ❑ *Ficha técnica de habitação* for post-30th March 2004 properties.
- ❑ *Cadernetas* (these should have your name and tax number on now and not the previous owners).
- ❑ Energy efficiency certificate.

Make sure that your property is registered at the land registry *(conservatória do registo predial)* as soon as possible after the final deed has been signed. **This is very important.**

Complaints

If you find yourself in the unfortunate position of having to make a complaint against your *solicitador(a)* or lawyer then you can do so by writing to their relevant governing bodies.

For lawyers go to the *Ordem dos Advogados* website at *www.oa.pt* and click on *Contactos* in the top right-hand side.

For *solicitadores* go to the *Câmara dos Solicitadores* website at *www.solicitador.net* and click on *Contactos* at the top and then on *Orgãos,* or on *Contacte-nos* in the top right-hand corner.

CASE STUDY: SIMON SHARP

Our move abroad had been semi-planned for about 10 years before it actually happened. Our first thoughts were to move to Spain, but prices rapidly moved from affordable to unrealistic.

That said, the Iberian Peninsula still retained its hold on us and so we looked into Portugal. Our initial research revealed a country that was steeped in tradition and family friendly, with a climate that appealed. We felt by now it was time to take definite steps towards the planned move abroad and decided to make a visit. Thanks to our eco-tourism business, we had a variety of great accommodation available to us and decided on a two-week stay in the Minho. Our initial feeling had been that Central Portugal was the place for us. However, after we arrived and explored, our minds were changed — it was the Minho for us.

We spent those initial two weeks in a hire car, going backwards and forwards and up and down the region, and finally settled on the area inland from Viana do Castelo. After deciding on our location, it was back to the UK, where we had 12 months to get everything ready to make the move. You can plan forever and wait for that perfect moment, but sometimes, life demands that you just do it and so we did!

Initially, I intended to develop business in Portugal for a UK-based solar panel manufacturer, having spent six months researching the market from the UK. All should have been ready to go, but then Portuguese bureaucracy reared its ugly head and it feels like we've been fighting that dragon ever since.

It soon became clear that, if we were going to create a successful business here, we could not rely on selling a single product in a saturated market. So we researched and selected a premium range of the most cost- effective equipment in renewable energy and Raiz Verde Lda was born.

Forming and running a business in Portugal is not for the faint-hearted. The costs are astronomical. Firstly, there is the requirement to have an accountant at approximately €250 per month, and then the seemingly random tax after random tax. You could be forgiven for thinking that, rather than supporting SME businesses, the Portuguese government is actively trying to put us out of business. If I knew then what I know now, would I form a business again? No chance! However, unless you're retiring on a pension, you need to make a living – and bear in mind there aren't enough jobs for the Portuguese, never mind foreign nationals unable to speak the language like a native.

To stand out as a business in Portugal is difficult. We took the view that our market should be Portuguese rather than expat. We concentrate on the quality of the product, providing what is right for the customer (not us) and back this up with exceptional customer service. There are many renewable energy businesses now in Portugal, some good, some not so good, and some with a double-glazing salesman approach. I believe those less ethical businesses will cease to trade as the market becomes more saturated. Grants, which were available for the installation of solar thermal, have been suspended for the moment and this has had a big impact on the cash flow of many renewable energy businesses. Renewable energy is still something of a luxury product here for property owners, but for those building new properties, solar thermal is now a requirement. However, a builder will often just use the cheapest equipment he can lay his hands on, unless instructed otherwise. It is a competitive, price-orientated market and there is always someone who can offer a cheaper product.

All that said, we love the area we live in and the children have settled in well to Portuguese school life, so the pros do outweigh the cons. I feel that a move to a country like Portugal is more appropriate for those with an independent income or an income that can be earned independent of location. Many expats think they can make some money in the tourism industry. Beware! There are a lot of accommodation providers in Portugal and even more rules and regulations. To have a legal tourism accommodation business costs a lot of money. To have an illegal one exposes you to an awful lot of risk and potential problems.

Overall, my advice would be to research the country and make sure it's right for you. Research the regions that appeal to you and make sure they have everything you want. Think about income. How are you really going to make a living? Vague ideas about tourism or teaching English (all schools now offer English as part of the curriculum) will just not be viable. The cost of living is not as cheap as you may think. Food and alcohol are certainly cheaper, but energy, insurance, telephone costs and so on are all more expensive. Property prices depend on the region. Our region, the Minho, is one of the more expensive areas and significantly more expensive than Central Portugal. Finally, if you do decide to start a business, then prepare yourself for bureaucracy and taxes.

All that said, it's a beautiful country!

Simon Sharp, the Minho, Northern Portugal

www.ethicalescape.com

www.raizverde.pt

Mortgages and Offshore Buyers

Until a few years ago, trying to obtain a mortgage in Portugal (especially if you were a foreigner) was extremely difficult.

However, things have moved on vastly and there now seem to be many banks and mortgage companies offering loans to purchase property in Portugal.

So, is it better to obtain your loan in the UK or Portugal? The answer probably depends on the interest rates and where you are receiving your income or where your money is kept. Interest rates on a Euro mortgage obtained in the UK, for example, are likely to be similar to those of a Portuguese mortgage, as most financial matters in Europe are connected to the Euribor and the interbank lending rate – *www.euribor-rates.eu*.

If you obtain a Portuguese mortgage and your money is mostly in the UK then you will have to consider the likely costs involved in transferring it. If you have most of your money in Portugal, however, or are working there, then this will not be an issue.

Whatever your situation seek reputable, qualified and independent financial advice before making a commitment to any loan – be it in the UK or Portugal.

Everyone's financial situation is different and while one can read general advice here and in other books, your circumstances are unique to you. The financial adviser should also preferably be someone who knows about Portuguese Law.

While mortgages now seem to be readily available to both foreign residents and non-residents different criteria will apply depending on how you are going to purchase your property.

It should be noted that, due to the amount of bad credit in Portugal, Portuguese banks do tend to be a little conservative in their attitude and have quite a low tolerance of risk.

You will have to show that you are in a strong financial position to gain approval and it can also take a long time to arrange, possibly up to three months! Although it has been known for people to obtain approval within a couple of weeks.

The first bank to arrange mortgage loans to British citizens, which could be secured on the property in Portugal, as opposed to a house in the UK, was Banco Totta, now Banco Santander Totta, in London. They started a specialist mortgage scheme in 1987 and are still one of the market leaders in this field. Other banks have since joined them.

Here is a list of some Portuguese banks offering mortgages:

- Millenium BCP: *www.millenniumbcp.pt*
- Banco Espirito Santo: *www.bes.pt*
- Banif: *www.banif.pt*
- Barclays Portugal: *www.barclays.pt*
- Santander Totta: *www.santandertotta.co.uk*
- Caixa Geral de Depositos: *www.cgd.pt*

In general, the maximum loan to value (LTV) is 80% of the purchase price for a period of up to 30 years (which must be completed by the age of 75) and a minimum loan of €50,000. However, some residents have managed to secure loans of up to 90% and more with guarantors. Once again, it all comes back down to the proof of your ability to pay and a proven track record.

There is generally a penalty for early repayment, which varies according to the type of mortgage, although some overpayments may be allowed.

Many banks and mortgage companies will recommend, or even insist, that life assurance is taken out — so that must also be considered in your costs, as well as the arrangement and valuation fees. Medical examinations are also usually required. These may be carried out in the UK or Portugal.

As well as lending money for a new build or resale property some banks will also consider loaning money for off plan stage payments.

The documents required in order to obtain a mortgage in Portugal are much the same as in the UK and other parts of Europe. These generally are:

- ❑ Pay slips and employer reference, if employed.
- ❑ Proof of income, if self-employed, or obtaining another source of income.
- ❑ Tax returns (P60 or equivalent).
- ❑ At least three months' bank statements and bank references.
- ❑ Certified copies of ID cards/passport.
- ❑ Fiscal/tax number.
- ❑ Utility bills.
- ❑ Property documents.

In 2003 the Portuguese government 'black-listed' certain places, like Gibraltar, for offshore property ownership. This led to a lot of people taking their money elsewhere and many with property in those places were led through an expensive maze, which either meant they moved their company to a 'non-black-listed' place like Delaware or Malta, or bought back their property onshore and paid the taxes.

There was a lot of wild speculation at the time and many people took advantage of the situation by charging fees to give advice and deal with people's affairs. Many people were panicked into making a decision to buy back their properties in their names and pay their dues.

Purchase tax *(IMT)* is currently 8% for a white-listed jurisdiction, but 15% for a black-listed jurisdiction. Council tax *(IMI)* is 5% for a black-listed jurisdiction and the same as onshore properties for a white-listed one.

Remember that an offshore company requires a fiscal representative, even if you are resident in Portugal, and you may have to pay additional fees if you rent out the property, such as when making an annual return, as well as for the general running of the company. Black-listed properties have to make an annual return regardless of whether they are rented out or not.

As with anything else financial, seek reputable, qualified advice before making a decision. It may or may not be beneficial to you to purchase a property offshore or from a Portuguese holding company. If you find a property you really like that is offshore, but you would prefer not to purchase it that way, then you can speak to the owners to see if they wish to bring it onshore first or transfer it to a Portuguese holding company.

What's What

As mentioned in the *Real Estate Agents & Vendors'* chapter, if you use a real estate agent in Portugal then copies of most of the following documents listed in this chapter should be in their possession. In addition, you should feel free to ask the agent or vendor for any copies if you have an interest in purchasing a property.

However, it may well be advisable to collect your own too as a safeguard. Your legal representative should also be able to supply copies at your request.

Land Registry – Conservatória do Registo Predial

The land registry (*conservatória do registo predial)* is where you can obtain copies of land registry certificates *(certidões de registo predial/certidões de teor)*. A land registry certificate will give you important information about the property you are interested in purchasing. It will tell you:

- ❑ Who the current owners are.
- ❑ Who has owned it previously.
- ❑ Whether there are any charges against the property, such as a mortgage *(hipoteca).*
- ❑ Whether there are any special conditions or rights on the property.
- ❑ The number of rooms, and what their functions are.

This certificate is a crucial document and should mirror the information contained in the *caderneta(s)* (see the *Tax Office — Serviço das Finanças* section in this chapter).

The deed *(escritura)* cannot be signed without a current (less than six months old) copy of this document.

The land registry certificate is also required for carrying out other property related matters, for example when seeking planning consent.

Visit the land registry in the area you are buying the property. To find the address go to *www.irn.mj.pt/IRN/sections/irn/contactos* and click on *Conservatórias de registo predial* under the *Serviços desconcentrados do IRN, I.P.* subheading. You can then download the file. This will give you a list of all the *conservatórias do registo predial* in Portugal.

You will need to know the title *(certidão)* number of the property, or at least the plot number of the land, to gain information.

Ask the person selling you the property for these details if you don't know them.

You can ask for either a simple copy *(uma cópia simples)* of the land registry certificate or an authenticated copy *(uma cópia autenticada)*. Simple copies are usually just a few Euros and are useful for initial enquiries. The authenticated copy, which costs considerably more, will have a cover and each page should be stamped with a seal.

Land registry certificates can also now be requested and paid for online, although only authenticated copies and not the cheaper simple versions. Go to *www.portaldocidadao.pt/PORTAL/pt/certidoes_online.* To set up a username and account click on *novo registo* in the top right hand corner.

If you use a legal representative then he/she should provide you with an authenticated copy after purchase and your purchase should be registered as soon as possible at this office after the final deed has been signed. It is not until the deed is registered at the land registry that you actually become the legal owner.

NATIVE'S TIP

It is advisable to visit the land registry on the day of completion (preferably with your legal representative, as they will usually be seen to more rapidly) to make one final check on any outstanding debts or for any new entries, which might affect your purchase.

Notary — Cartório Notarial

The notary *(cartório notarial)* is not only the place where you will sign your final deed *(escritura)* but also where you can obtain copies of previous deeds.

Unfortunately, obtaining copies of previous deeds isn't always easy. Although a person is likely to sign a deed at the notary closest to the property they are buying this isn't always the case. In fact, a person can sign a deed at any notary in Portugal. If a legal representative cannot find a slot at the nearest notary he/she might call all the others in the area to see which ones have available dates. They might also liaise with the legal representative on the other side (if there is one) to go to the notary most convenient for both of them.

Apparently, there are no central records for deeds in Portugal, which also doesn't help, but you should be able to find out when and where previous deeds were signed by asking at the nearest land registry *(conservatória do registo predial)* to the property. This office, as well as the tax office (*serviço das finanças*), requires a copy as proof of the change of ownership.

To find out where a particular notary is situated go to *www.irn.mj.pt/IRN/sections/irn/contactos* and click on *Cartórios Notariais* under the *Serviços desconcentrados do IRN, I.P.* subheading. You can then download the two files. This will give you a list of all the public (*públicos*) and private (*privados*) notaries in Portugal.

Not so long ago many notaries became private, so the prices to get copies of deeds and other notarised documents has risen substantially.

However, it is well worth trying to get hold of the current property owner's deed, as well as the land registry certificate (*certidão de registo predial/teor*) in order to confirm that they are, in fact, the owner. It should be filed under their name (or a company name in the case of offshore owners and Portuguese holding companies).

Knowing the date that the current owner bought the property will also help to locate it in the event that they have records of more than one deed in that name.

The deed will state the declared price of the property and the purchase tax *(IMT)* document number. A copy of this tax document is kept in the file with the deed and will show when it was paid. You can also get a copy of this from the local tax office *(serviço das finanças)*.

Upon signing your final deed, details of the purchase tax paid and copies of the following must be presented to the notary: *certidão de registo predial/teor* (less than six months old), the *caderneta(s)* (less than one year old), either a habitation licence *(licença de habitação)* or a pre-1951 certificate *(pre-1951 certidão)*, a *ficha técnica de habitação* (for properties built after March 30th 2004) and an energy efficiency certificate.

Fiscal numbers *(números de contribuinte)* and identification documents (passport, residence card or ID card numbers and details) also have to be provided.

If you use a legal representative then he/she should provide you with an authenticated copy of the deed and purchase tax document soon after purchase.

The final deed is usually signed between one to three months after signing the promissory contract *(contrato de promessa de compra e venda)*. All the parties involved must agree this date. See the *Professional Legal Advice* chapter for more details on what should appear on both the promissory contract and the final deed, and for more information on power of attorney.

The notary's (*notário(a)*) job is to check that all the documentation is present, that the purchase tax has been paid, to read the deed out loud to all those present and to witness the signing after all the parties have agreed that they have understood and accepted the terms of the document.

If you do not understand Portuguese, you will be required to provide a translator. Your legal representative can carry out this function, if they speak English, but it is often a good idea to use a qualified, independent translator.

NATIVE'S TIP

It is wise to check the property before signing the final deed, as you buy it in that condition, and not in the condition as when you first saw it and signed the promissory contract. Check that the vendor hasn't taken anything that you were expecting to be left, or replaced fixed units, such as kitchen and bathroom equipment, with inferior quality ones. Do not go through with the sale unless you are completely satisfied, as it will be extremely difficult to seek any redress later.

Check with your legal representative on your rights if you have any doubts before proceeding.

Casa Pronta

Since around 2006, the Portuguese government has been implementing an initiaive called *SIMPLEX*. The idea is to simplify and cut down on bureaucracy. There have been various acts introduced, one notable one being a new service called *Casa Pronta* – *www.casapronta.pt*.

Casa Pronta (literally — 'Ready House') allows people to do everything related to the buying and selling of urban properties at a single counter in the land registry office (*conservatória do registo predial*), or at some branches of citizens' shops (*lojas do cidadão*) where there are land registry desks. For example, payment of the taxes involved, contracts for buying and selling, *IMI* exemption requests and all the necessary registrations.

You can use this service whether you need bank credit or not. Final deeds (*escrituras*) are also no longer compulsory.

It is hoped that this will reduce costs and simplify the bureaucratic procedures involved in property acquisition and transfer of ownership.

The *Casa Pronta* service is also now available at some banks and there is currently a trial running with a few real estate agents. Therefore, it will not always be necessary to go to a land registry office.

While this new initiative may interest some, especially those with a strong grasp of the Portuguese language, there have been some teething problems with the service. It is probably still advisable for foreign buyers to seek the services of a legal representative and to use the more traditional route involving a notary.

Tax Office — Serviço das Finanças

The local tax office *(serviço das finanças)* is where you obtain your fiscal number *(número de identificação fiscal or NIF)*, also known as *número do contribuinte*, in order to open a bank account and buy property in Portugal.

If you are a non-resident, then under Portuguese law you will need to appoint a fiscal representative to go along with you and sign that they are responsible for any payments/debts in Portugal and to make sure that you meet your tax and financial obligations.

A fiscal representative could be anyone in theory but is usually a legal representative, financial adviser or accountant, as the responsibilities are quite onerous.

You will need to take ID, a passport for example, and your details will then be entered onto a computer database along with those of your fiscal representative, if required. An A4 sheet showing these details and your fiscal number will then be printed out and given to you.

In the past, plastic cards with your fiscal number on were sent by post to your fiscal address for you to sign and keep with you. However, due to current changes to ID cards for Portuguese citizens, in favour of the new, all-in-one, 'super' ID card, which hasn't yet been introduced for foreign EU citizens, you may now no longer receive a card. Therefore, you should memorise this number or carry it with you at all times, as you will be surprised at how many times you will be asked for this number when doing various things in Portugal.

The local tax office is also the place where you can obtain copies of *cadernetas*. *Caderneta* literally means 'exercise book' but in relation to property it is like a 'log book' showing details of the property and its rateable value. The full title of this document is *caderneta predial*.

There are two types of *caderneta predial*: urban *(urbana)* and rustic *(rústica)*. If you buy a house on a plot in an urbanisation, then you will only have a *caderneta urbana* whereas if you buy a house with land in the countryside, you should have both. It is known as a mixed property (*prédio misto*). They will give a detailed description of the property.

The urban *caderneta* will show such information as:

- Identification (*identificação do prédio*) and localisation (*localização do prédio*) of the property — district (*distrito*), council (*concelho*) and parish (*freguesia*) — as well as the street name and urbanisation or locale.
- Article number (*artigo matricial*).
- The neighbours (*confrontações*).
- A description of the property (*descrição do prédio*) — the number of rooms in the property and what they consist of.

- The rateable value of the property (*valor patrimonial*).
- The owner's name (*nome*), address for correspondence (*morada*) and fiscal number (*identificação fiscal*).

The rustic *caderneta* will show information, such as:

- Identification (*identificação do prédio*) and localisation (*localização do prédio*) of the property; district (*distrito*), council (*concelho*) and parish areas (*freguesia*).
- Map section (*secção*) letter(s) and article number (*artigo matricial Nº*).
- Land measurements.
- How the parcels (*parcelas*) are divided up and the types of tree culture on the land.
- The rateable value of the property (*valor patrimonial*).
- The owner's name (*nome*), address for correspondence (*morada*) and fiscal number (*identificação fiscal*).
- Any alterations (under *observações*) to the land size, e.g. detachments or annexations.
- A map should also be attached showing the neighbours and boundaries.

Only the actual owner or a legal representative can ask for copies, so before proceeding with a purchase ask the owner and/or legal representative to get you copies so you can see exactly what is on them.

Check whether the details on the *caderneta(s)* are consistent with the land registry certificate *(certidão de registo predial/teor)*. They should be. A final deed (*escritura*) cannot be signed without current (less than one year old) copies of this document.

Once a homeowner, you can also obtain copies of *cadernetas* online at the *Portal das Finanças* website *www.portaldasfinancas.gov.pt*. Go to *Serviços* on the left-hand side and then *Consultar*. Scroll down to *Imovéis* in the list and click on *Património Predial*.

In order to register to use the site, go to *novo utilizador* in the right-hand column. Fill in your details, i.e. fiscal number (*Nº Contribuinte*), email, telephone (*telefone*), fiscal address (*Morada Fiscal*) and a security question (*Pergunta*) and answer (*Resposta*). Submit by clicking on *Pedir Senha* at the bottom. You will then be sent a password in the mail to your fiscal address in Portugal (which could be that of your fiscal representaive).

One other matter that may concern you in relation to this department and your property purchase is obtaining an exemption from paying your rates (*imposto municipal sobre imóveis — IMI*) once you have completed. This only applies to those who will be resident in Portugal and using the property as their principal residence. You may want to ask your legal representative to carry this out as part of their purchasing duties on your behalf. It should be done within 60 days of purchase.

You can also now request this online at the above website by going to *Serviços,* followed by *Entregar, Declarações, IMI* and *Pedido de Isenção.*

The Portuguese government recently extended the period of exemption for payment of *IMI*. The initiative aims to help families minimise the costs associated with owning a home.

At the time of writing, those with a property *valor patrimonial* of up to €157,500 will be given an eight year exemption and those with a property *valor patrimonial* of between €157,500 and €236,250 will be given a four year exemption. This does not apply to properties owned by an offshore company.

Documents needed to obtain this exemption include:

- ❑ Fiscal Nº.
- ❑ Deed (*escritura*).
- ❑ Residency certificate/card.
- ❑ Request form.

NATIVE'S TIP

While as a non-resident you have to appoint a fiscal representative to be responsible for your financial affairs in Portugal, they do not have to pay your bills for you. Most fiscal representatives will charge a fee for doing this and so it may be cheaper for you to pay them yourself via Internet banking or direct debit. All your fiscal representative then needs to do is to forward you the bills.

Habitation Licence, Pre-1951 Certificate and Ficha Técnica de Habitação

Before purchasing any property, the seller must provide you with either a habitation licence *(licença de habitação)* or a pre-1951 certificate *(pre-1951 certidão).*

Without one of these documents, you cannot legally buy the property and live in it. You can obtain copies of these at the local council *(câmara municipal).*

You may also see the term utilisation licence (*licença de utilização).* Although they are sometimes used interchangeably, the habitation licence usually refers to a building suitable for habitation whereas the utilisation licence refers to buildings for other uses, such as shops.

The builder or responsible architect will ask the local council for a habitation licence when a property construction has been completed. The council will then usually make an inspection known as a *vistória.* If the building has been completed to the correct specifications and building regulations, then a habitation licence is issued (also see *Builders & Architects'* chapter).

A pre-1951 certificate proves that the building was constructed before August 7th 1951 and, therefore, does not require a habitation licence. Pre-1951 properties that have had work done to them *will* require a habitation licence (and more recently a *ficha técnica de habitação*).

To obtain a pre-1951 certificate the owner has to provide the following to the local council:

- ❑ A set of topographical plans.
- ❑ Photographs.
- ❑ Property documents.
- ❑ Statement of two local witnesses.

If you buy an old property with a pre-1951 certificate and then carry out works to renovate it after gaining building permission, you will need to apply for a habitation licence when the works are completed. You, your builder or architect must apply for this at the local council.

Properties built after March 30th 2004 now also need a *ficha técnica de habitação* (*FTH*). This gives detailed technical information on the property in terms of construction type and the suppliers and materials used. It has been referred to as a building's 'ID card'.

The builder must supply this document to the local council and it must be presented to the notary by the seller or real estate agent at the time of the final deed signing. The seller or real estate agent should also provide you with a copy on request. You can get copies of this document at the local council.

Utilities

One of the most important things you will need to know is how the property you intend to buy gets its water.

Is it from the local council *(câmara municipal)*, or does it have its own borehole *(furo)*, or well *(poço)*? Do you have to buy your supply from a neighbour, or does the local fire service *(bombeiros)* deliver it to a water tank *(cisterna)* on the property?

Without some form of water supply the property will obviously not be habitable and virtually worthless.

You may be told that the property currently gets its water from a neighbour but that the local council are planning to install mains water in the area, or that you can apply to connect to the mains supply yourself. If this is the case then do not take somebody's word for it – go to the local council to check the likely costs involved as it could be quite expensive.

Also, remember that a neighbour could in the future change his/her mind about supplying you with water, so this needs to be carefully considered.

If the property has a well then you would be very wise to see it in the bone dry summer months as well as the wetter winter ones to ensure it doesn't dry up.

If there is a borehole then is it only for your use or shared? When was the borehole pump last maintained and how old is it? What are the likely costs involved in maintaining it?

If there is a water tank, what is its condition like? Is a water quality check advisable?

If you buy a property with a borehole then you should check that it has an up-to-date licence with the *Ministério do Ambiente, do Ordenamento do Território e do*

Desenvolvimento Regional. See the following websites for the nearest office:

North: *www.ccr-norte.pt/ccrn/contacto.php*

(Direct link to the contact page.)

Central: *www.ccdrc.pt*

(Click on *CCDRC* and then on *Contactos,* both on the left-hand side, or go to the extreme bottom of the home page and click on *Contactos.*)

Lisbon and Tagus Valley: *www.ccdr-lvt.pt*

(Click on *Contactos* on the left-hand side at the very bottom.)

Alentejo: *www.ccdr-a.gov.pt*

(Click on *Contacte*-nos in the left-hand column.)

Algarve: *www.ccdr-alg.pt*

(Click on *Contactos* at the very top.)

The licence is called an *Alvará de Licença de Captação de Águas Subterrânea.* A borehole licence needs to be renewed on its expiry, which is usually every five years. Since 2007 this renewal is now free.

Rural properties will not be on mains drainage so check that the property has a septic tank *(fossa)* and if not, if it is feasible to install one. If there is already one there, have its condition assessed.

At the time of writing both boreholes and septic tanks, which empty into the water table or soil, were also being required to be registered with another authority called the *ARH* (*Admministração da Região Hidrográfica*) under a law introduced back in May 2007. Springs, rivers, dams, reservoirs, lakes, ponds and wells on property must also be registered under this law. Check that this has been carried out.

Regional offices for the *ARH* are as follows:

North: *www.arhnorte.pt*

(Click on *Contactos* at very bottom on the right.)

Central: *www.arhcentro.pt*

(Click on *Contactos* on the right-hand side.)

Lisbon and Tagus Valley: *www.arhtejo.pt*

(Click on *Contactos* at very bottom in the middle.)

Alentejo: *www.arhalentejo.pt*

(Click on *Coloque as suas questões under Contacte-nos* in the left hand column.)

Algarve: *www.arhalgarve.pt*

(Click on *Contactos* at the top on the right.)

If you are buying a ruin on a plot of land which you wish to renovate, and which is without electricity, then check with the electricity company *(EDP)* that you will be able to connect and if so, how much it will cost. The *EDP* website is at *www.edp.pt/pt*. The website does have an English translation, however this gives only limited information. It is therefore recommended that the website is used in Portuguese to get full usage of the services it provides.

Don't just take a real estate agent's word that you will get electricity quickly and easily. Always check. If a property has never had electricity, it will be a much longer and trickier procedure, as the building must be up to a certain habitable standard to receive permission for a connection to be made. If it is not to the required standard, then work would have to be carried out to make sure that it is.

Also check how far the property is from the nearest electrical post. These are usually sited every 100 metres and as it costs around €1000 for each post, it could work out quite expensive to get electricity to the property.

If there is no phone line to the property then check with *Portugal Telecom (PT)* if it will be possible to install one and the likely costs and timescale involved. The *PT* website is at *www.telecom.pt*.

Likewise, check with the various Internet service providers that you will be able to connect to broadband, if you need Internet access. Here are some Internet service providers' websites:

- *http://net.sapo.pt*
- *http://acesso.clix.pt*
- *www.cabovisao.pt*
- *www.oni.pt*
- *www.meo.pt*
- *www.zon.pt*

If the property you are interested in buying already has a line and telephone number then you can insert the number in the box marked *verificar cobertura* or *confirme cobertura* on the websites mentioned above to see if Internet access is possible in the location and if so, what type of connection.

Some sites also allow you to type in the postal code *(código postal)* of the area to check for coverage.

Check that all utility bills are paid in full before the final deed signing or you could become liable for any debts.

After purchase, make sure that all the contracts are changed over into your name. If you have agreed with your legal representative to do this on your behalf, as part of their paid duties, then make sure that they carry this task out.

Take readings from the meters so that you can check any bills you later receive. Most bills are now bimonthly and estimated so make sure that proper readings are done and logged.

If you register with the *EDP* website above, you can also set up contracts, provide accurate meter readings, change tariffs and carry out various other services online. To do this click on *edpOnline* in the left-hand column of the homepage and when you are taken to the next page click on *Registar* at the top on the right.

Finally, be prepared for the fact that things often move very slowly in Portugal and you will need a lot of patience in dealing with most authorities, utilities and businesses. If you are a very impatient person, or get stressed over the slightest thing, then consider very carefully if Portugal is the place for you.

NATIVE'S TIP

Some of the websites in this chapter have an option to view in English. However, if you wish to contact them by email, telephone or letter, and do not speak Portuguese, then arrange for an independent Portuguese speaker to do this on your behalf. If you write in English, it is unlikely that you will receive a reply.

Also, free translators on the Internet are not very accurate and normally only give you a literal translation. These are, therefore, best avoided for translating serious and crucial emails, documents and letters.

Energy Efficiency Certificate

Since 1st January 2009 it has been obligatory for residences in Portugal to have an energy efficiency certificate for the selling process or for renting.

These certificates have to be passed by a technician (*perito qualificado* – *PQ*) recognised by the Energy Agency (*ADENE*). To find the contact details of technicians qualified to pass these certificates you can consult the agency's website at *www.adene.pt*.

Click on *Entidade Gestora* on the left-hand side, then *Bolsa de Peritos* and *Pesquisa*, also on the left-hand side.

You can then select the region (*Região*), district (*Distrito*) and council area (*Concelho*), and finally *Pesquisa na Bolsa de Peritos Qualificados* at the bottom right for a list of names in your area.

You can also check if someone claiming to be a technician is in fact qualified by entering their registration number (*Nº de Perito*) and clicking on *Pesquisa na Bolsa de Peritos Qualificados.*

This certificate must be shown to the notary at the time of the final deed signing.

Swimming Pool Licences

In the last couple of years regulations concerning the building of swimming pools have changed slightly. It used to be that any swimming pool *(piscina)* had to have both a construction licence *(licença de construção)* and a utilisation licence *(licença de utilização)* from the local council *(câmara municipal)* and these could take some time to obtain.

It now seems that in urban locations things are a little more flexible. According to a new law introduced in 2008, in some instances it will not be necessary to advise the local council. However, it is always best to check either directly with the local planning department or with a local architect about any works you wish to carry out to your property in order to be on the safe side.

The architect who prepares the project for the swimming pool will have to check that a pool is allowed in the area in which you wish to build it and that it falls within the rules of the *PDM* (see the *Real Estate Agents & Vendors'* chapter for more on the *PDM*). The project will then be submitted to the local council under what is known as a *comunicação prévia*. They have 30 days to respond.

If they do not respond within the 30 day period then you have tacit approval to go ahead with the building works. However, if the local council has to consult a third party then they are allowed more time.

In areas known as *RAN* (agricultural land) or *REN* (ecological land) you will find it extremely difficult, if not impossible, to gain permission for a swimming pool. So check first to avoid disappointment!

There are a lot of illegal swimming pools in Portugal so double check on this. If you don't then you could end up inheriting a substantial fine due to its unauthorised construction. The swimming pool should also appear on the land registry certificate *(certidão de registo predial/teor)*, map and *caderneta*.

Maps

Maps of the property you intend to buy and its boundaries can be found at the local council *(câmara municipal)*.

You will need to know the plot number (usually one or two letters followed by a number, e.g. BQ157) and the parish *(freguesia)* it falls under.

Copies of these maps usually cost just a few Euros and you can purchase maps of varying scales and types.

Some of the local councils, however, have very old maps, which have not been updated for many years.

To obtain more up to date maps, go to the nearest Portuguese Geography Institute (*Instituto Geográfico Português – IGEO*) in the region, or order via their website by visiting *www.igeo.pt* and clicking on *localização* at the top for the address and details of the various regional offices. Click on *produtos*, back on the homepage, for the various things you can order. They also keep records of ownership and details of the history of the plot, for example if it has been split up or merged with another plot in the past.

Alternatively, you can go here to view maps online: *www.igeo.pt/servicos/cic/cad_seccoes.asp*. Just enter your district (*Distrito*), council (*Concelho*), parish council (*Freguesia*) and plot section letters (*Secção*) and click on *Seleccionar* to view. You can zoom in and out and move up and down as you need.

CASE STUDY: DONNA & PETER NUTTER

The decision to move to Portugal came when my husband, Pete, and I found that we were spending less and less time together as a family. This was largely due to work and the demands of the transport company Pete owned with his father, which involved long hours and a lot of stress. His parents had been contemplating buying a property abroad in order to spend the winters away and so Pete and I, who also wanted out of the rat race, decided to join them in looking at a move overseas. We also looked at moving to the countryside within the UK.

After looking at various options and countries and not finding exactly what we wanted, Pete's parents came back from their annual holiday in the Algarve. They informed us that property wasn't quite as expensive as they had expected and asked if we fancied giving it a go over there. We started our research and checked on various websites and forums to get background information regarding the possible pitfalls and negatives, as well as the advantages of relocating there.

After this, Pete, his father and uncle went to Portugal for a week and viewed potential properties and businesses. Anyone considering a move to Portugal has to realise that without fluency in the language or a specific qualification and/or an internet-run business you are limited as to what work you can do. We didn't have the language skills and so, after careful consideration, we opted for a resort/holiday business.

We purchased a licence for a café/snack bar and opened up doing English breakfasts and snacks. Besides the sales reps and council officials, everyone we dealt with was English. This made it a lot easier to run the business. However, one word of warning if you are considering doing this: take into consideration that, due to the business being seasonal, you must save during the summer or you will not be able to survive in the winter months.

We purchased the licence in December 2005 and ran the café from a rented property, so that, if for any reason we were not able to stay or couldn't make a living in the Algarve, we would not have put all our money into the business. This turned out to be a good choice. Other people we got to know had purchased businesses with larger *trespasses* and fees, only to find local rules change on how properties could be sold. As a result, their properties were virtually worthless to sell in comparison to what had been paid for them.

There were seven of us that moved altogether. Pete's mum and dad moved in December 2005 to open the snack bar, and after waiting in the UK to sell property and tie up loose ends, Pete, his uncle, our two children and I followed in August 2006. With all of us more or less moving together, we had a natural support network. We also came to meet many other expats and locals who became our friends and helped us along the way.

We bought the business in a tourist resort for ease of language. However, when it came to buying our property, we wanted to be out of the resort and among a more Portuguese community. Our children would be going to a Portuguese school and we wanted to integrate as much as possible if this was going to be our home.

Our daughter, who was then four years old, was registered at a local nursery school and our son, then seven, was registered at a local primary school. Portugal seems to thrive on red tape and the process was not a particularly easy one! However, our estate agent was a guardian angel and helped us with registering the children for school, as well as with all the medical requirements that accompany this — in the first six months of living here both children had to have eight injections. (BCG/tuberculosis is compulsory in Portugal from birth; in the UK this is usually given around the age of 13, if at all.)

Our estate agent also helped us arrange our fiscal (tax) cards, various property papers, and came to parents' evening!

As in the UK, you receive a national insurance card just before your sixteenth birthday, which means you automatically registered for everything. However, if you are new, you have to start from the beginning and make various trips to register and get everything you need.

After about one year, the children had the language more or less under control and had settled into Portuguese school life. We had also found a local bar that we loved only 50 metres from our apartments and felt at home going there, and meeting and chatting to local people.

The snack bar paid its bills and fed the family, but it could never really provide a wage to support five adults and two children, so I got a job as a kids' club rep in a local hotel for the summer and Pete's uncle got some bar work in the evenings.

As we were a large family, we purchased a people carrier and Pete began to get asked to help transport people to and from the airport. It became apparent that this could be a potential new business. It took two years to get the final licence, which meant yet more red tape and bureaucracy, but we finally got the business, Algarve 365, up and running in December 2008. We now have 10 drivers (all British expats living in Portugal) covering the whole of the Algarve and specialise in private airport and golf transfers.

We closed the bar in October 2008 at the end of the season.

Regrets? None! We love our life here and the only thing I miss is my family back in the UK. However, as is the case when living somewhere as beautiful as Portugal, we are never short of visitors! So I probably see more of them now than before.

It has to be said that not being fluent in the language is an issue at times and the bureaucracy can be a little wearing. Nothing ever happens immediately here, and especially when you are desperate for it to! Portugal is a relaxed and laidback country, and the Portuguese hold family values in high regard and enjoy nothing more than socialising and supporting each other.

We wanted a slower pace of life where we could be a family and enjoy more time together and this, especially in the winter months, is exactly what we've achieved.

Donna & Peter Nutter, Portimão, Algarve

www.algarve-365.com

Condominiums

If you buy an apartment, a townhouse or house on a private condominium *(condomínio)* then you will obviously have to pay community fees (*gastos de comunidade*) for the maintenance of communal areas.

These fees might include such things as:

- Gardens and grounds
- Swimming pools
- Lighting
- Painting
- Cleaning
- Insurance
- Administration

These charges are calculated on the basis of each owner's share in the development or apartment block, and this percentage should be written in the deed. The condominium will also have a set of rules and restrictions.

Therefore, it is wise to obtain a copy of the rules and restrictions and do some research regarding the management before agreeing to purchase a property on a condominium.

A condominium usually has a paid administrator and by law there has to be an annual meeting (AGM). This is held before mid January. At the AGM the administrator must show the expenditure against the budget that was approved for the previous year, set a new budget and seek approval for the administrator for the coming year. If you are unable to attend, you can usually make a proxy vote.

Check that the fees for the property have been paid up to date so that you do not become liable for them after the purchase. It is now mandatory for a vendor to provide this information to a potential buyer, so make sure you ask the question.

Also, make sure to check the minutes of annual meetings and previous charges to help determine if any additional charges due to maintence work are likely, or if fees are likely to rise substantially. This is especially important in the case of older, more run-down properties.

If possible, speak to other owners already living there to get an idea of the community and how it is run.

Under a new law, condominium companies must have public liability insurance, which should cover anything related to the condominium administration.

There must also be a bank account (which can be a savings or investment account) set up as a reservation fund, in addition to a day-to-day bank account, necessary for maintenance and other works that are required from time to time. It is called a *fundo comum de reserva* and should be at least 10% of the owners' contributions.

The administrator must make any information available regarding this and other bank accounts set up for the condominium on request.

For more information on condominium legislation you can consult a very useful website at *www.gestaodocondominio.pt*. However, it is currently only available in Portuguese. Click on *Administração* and then *Legislação* on the left-hand side.

Summary: Top Ten BuyingTips

1. Think very carefully about your reasons for buying a property in Portugal and/or relocating. Do your homework thoroughly, especially if you need to work and/or have children to consider. Take your time and don't rush into things!
2. Rent if possible before relocating permanently, in order to make sure that the area, or even the country, is right for you. Consider renting out your home in your country of origin first before selling up lock, stock and barrel.
3. Choose your own independent and fully qualified legal advice and avoid using the legal representatives put forward by a real estate agent, builder or vendor.
4. Be careful who you use to introduce you to properties and vendors. Check out their credentials and where applicable, their qualifications and any governing body/company registrations.
5. Only use qualified and properly registered builders and architects – preferably recommended from an independent source. View their previous work before engaging them.

6. Do your own property document gathering and checks, alongside any legal help you may choose to use. Get a map of the property and its boundaries, and the area.
7. Do not evade tax or do anything else untoward. This might cost you much more than you saved in the long run!
8. Seek independent financial advice from a reputable and qualified source before parting with any money in Portugal. Let them help you plan properly and throroughly for your relocation and/or retirement abroad.
9. Learn as much Portuguese as you can and use independent translators for any important document signings, so that you know exactly what you are agreeing to.
10. Do only as you would feel comfortable doing in your home country and don't cut important corners to avoid expense. You may regret it later!

Selling a Property

Although this book is mostly concerned with buying a property in Portugal, I feel it necessary to also make some mention about selling a property.

It is a fact of life that some people may wish to return to where they came from, move to another country, or simply move elsewhere within Portugal at a later stage.

The first thing you need to decide on is whether you are going to use a real estate agent or to sell privately. In addition, you will also need to decide on whom your market is going to be. Will it be native or foreign, or perhaps both?

To sell privately, the simplest thing you can do is to put a for sale (*vende-se*) sign on your property, but be warned, as well as prospective buyers contacting you, so will a number of real estate agents touting for your business.

At this stage, you should also consider how attractive your property looks to potential buyers. Unless you are just selling a ruin for renovation, presentation of your property is obviously of vital importance.

First impressions are crucial, both in relation to the exterior and interior. A property that appears to have been cared for will tend to sell quicker, and often for more, than one that has been neglected and left to fall into disrepair. You should consider seemingly minor things that can make a big difference, such as repairing broken gates and tiles, and cleaning paintwork, shutters and windows. Go round your home with a critical eye, and remove as much junk and clutter as possible to give people a feel for what it might be like if it was their home.

While not spending vast amounts of money that you may never recoup, you many want to consider replacing a few items, such as worn out kitchen units or bathroom suites, to give it more appeal. Simple things like a few flowers dotted around the rooms, soft music, adequate lighting and the smell of freshly brewed coffee may make your home seem more attractive to potential buyers.

After placing a for sale sign on your property, the next step might be to place advertisements in classified sections of newspapers and magazines (UK and/or Portuguese depending on your market) on Internet forums, on free property websites, Facebook Marketplace and on other existing property websites.

However, note that newspaper and magazine classifieds tend to be very expensive, as do some websites.

If you decide to set up your own website to advertise your property, then you must be sure that you will get enough people viewing it. How are you going to do this? Are you able to design the site or will you have to pay someone else to design it for you?

If this all seems like too much work and hassle then you will need to approach one or several real estate agents. They will usually have expert knowledge of the market, the necessary contacts, an established website and also the marketing know how that you might lack.

Getting recommendations from others who have sold is also an extremely good idea, as some agents are excellent, while others are a complete waste of time.

Once you have some recommendations then you should check out their credentials and qualifications just as you would for buying. Read the *Real Estate Agents & Vendors'* chapter to refresh your memory on how to go about doing this using the *INCI* website – *www.inci.pt*.

Real estate agents in Portugal charge high commissions. These are usually in the range of 3% to 6%. Negotiate with agents to see if you can get the percentage reduced. However, bear in mind that the more agents you have marketing your property, the less likely they are to agree to a lower percentage.

Some agents request exclusive rights, but tying yourself down to an exclusive deal for a fixed period of time will not enhance your chances of getting a quick sale so it is usually better to have your property on the market with several real estate agents.

It also makes sense to go with agents who advertise in different places and who use different methods including the web in order to give your property a lot more marketing exposure.

Like everything else, a property has a market value and you must ask a realistic price if you wish to get a quick sale.

Listen to your real estate agent's advice and look around at equivalent properties for sale in your area to get a feel for what you should be asking for.

With regard to the agreed asking price, keep a close eye on what your property is being marketed for on agents' websites and portfolios. It is not unheard of for an agent to agree a price with a vendor but then to go away and inflate it substantially in order to get more commission.

Once you have decided on which agents you are going to put your property on the market with, you will be asked to sign a contract known as a *contrato de mediação*. This will state the terms of agreement, details of the property, the price you are seeking, the commission to be paid and when it is to be paid.

Make sure that you get the Portuguese version of this contract translated into English by an independent translator so that you know exactly what you are agreeing to.

With regard to when the commission is paid, it has been known for some agents to ask for this immediately after they have found you a buyer and the promissory contract has been signed. However, in the unlikely event that the buyer pulls out before the final deed signing, you will be faced with the prospect of having to pay another commission when another buyer for your property is found.

Therefore, it is advisable to pay any commission due after the final deed has been signed and not before. Make sure that this is stated in the *contrato de mediação* and ask the agent for a proper invoice *(factura)* for the commission before handing over any money.

The process and legal requirements for selling a property in Portugal are similar to buying, especially in terms of the documentation.

Your real estate agent has a duty to obtain up to date copies of all documentation and to check that all is legitimate and correct before putting your property on the market.

You will need to work in conjunction with your agent to make sure that this is carried out. Be certain that you have no outstanding charges, for example rates (*IMI*) against the property or this could delay the sale by many months.

Remember that once you have agreed a price for the sale and signed a promissory contract that any backing out on your part will mean that you have to pay the purchaser double the deposit they have put down.

Also make sure that if a real estate agent is involved in the selling of the property that their name and details appear on the final deed *(escritura)*. This is now required by law, so don't agree to any deal to have their name left off, in order to save them paying tax on the commission.

Any fixtures and fittings you wish to sell in the property must be agreed separately with the purchaser and should not be included in the property price.

Lastly, in relation to the sale there is the issue of capital gains tax (*imposto sobre mais valia*).

If you own a home in Portugal, which is your principal residence, then on the sale of that property you must roll the money over onto another property in the EU within two years (or up to one year before the sale) or face capital gains tax. If you do not rollover the money, then you will pay tax on 50% of the gain made. Note that the gain will be calculated on the basis of what was declared on your deed *(escritura)* when you purchased and what is declared on the deed when you sell.

If you sell within five years of purchase then you can offset any improvements you have made to the property by producing the invoices *(facturas)* – hence why it is important to ask for invoices from those who work for you and pay the VAT (*IVA*).

You must declare the gain on your next personal income tax (*IRS*) declaration after the sale. After any adjustments 50% of the gain will then be added to any other income you have made during that year and taxed at marginal rates.

Non-residents selling a property face an automatic 25% tax rate on the total gain made. There is no rollover.

Speak to a reputable financial adviser to ascertain what your likely tax burden will be.

Renting

Renting can be seen from two different perspectives:

1. Renting somewhere while you are researching your relocation and looking to buy a property.
2. Renting out a property you own, in order to make some income.

In this chapter I will look at both holiday rentals and long-term rentals. However, before doing so, I would like to offer some words of caution with regard to renting out your property. If the only means of supporting your venture, in terms of paying a mortgage, is to receive regular rental income, then please do some thorough research.

Real estate agents will often advise potential buyers that they will have absolutely no problems in renting out their property after purchase, especially for holiday lets. However, this is getting increasingly hard to do. Many renters are becoming buyers and the holiday rental market is extremely competitive.

This is not only the case within Portugal, but also in Europe and worldwide, as many more holiday destinations are opening up to the public.

If you cannot support your buying venture without renting out your property then think very carefully as to whether you should be doing it in the first place. It could be a big risk!

Long-Term Rental

Long-term rentals are more easily found in cities and bigger towns, although it is possible to find them elsewhere.

The properties will not usually be furnished *(sem móveis)*, unless in resort areas, and utilities are rarely included. Rents will vary considerably, according to the area and the size of the property and the facilities on offer. In cities and large towns rents can be very high in relation to salaries.

The minimum period for commercial rental is currently five years. There are exceptions to this, i.e. for educational or professional reasons and tourism.

A contract can be for one year or sometimes less, but it then becomes a rental agreement rather than a legal rental contract.

If you sign a written legal contract *(contrato de arrendamento)* it should be witnessed and notarised.

If you do not speak good Portuguese then you should get this contract translated by an independent translator so you know exactly what you are agreeing to before signing.

The landlord and tenant must each sign an original copy and a third copy should be given to the local tax office *(serviço das finanças)*. The contract should include:

- ❑ The landlord and tenant's ID details.
- ❑ The identification of the property and its location.
- ❑ The habitation licence *(licença de habitação)* details.
- ❑ The date and duration of the contract.
- ❑ The amount of rent per month.

Other information may also be added to the contract, if agreed between the landlord and the tenant. This might include such things as the state of the building and its contents at the time of rental, who is responsible for any repairs and maintenance, the rules and regulations for the condominium (if applicable) and any other restrictions.

A landlord must also have a basic buildings insurance policy and the tenant should take out his or her own personal contents insurance.

After signing the contract, the tenant then has to pay the first month's rent, plus a deposit, which is usually of the same amount.

Rent increases are allowed as follows:

- Contracts less than eight years – annually by an amount determined by the government.

- Contracts more than eight years – the means of calculating the annual increase can be specified in the contract.
- As a result of any building works and improvements the landlord is required to make by the local council (*câmara municipal*) the rent can be increased in accordance with the value of the works.

A landlord and tenant may agree to terminate a rental contract at any time and this should normally be done in writing. Outside of this, the law specifies different periods of notice for terminating an agreement or contract. These are between three months and one year, depending on the type and length of the contract.

A tenant can terminate the contract at any time if the landlord does not fulfil their conditions and may also request compensation.

A landlord can request to have a tenant evicted via the courts for the following:

- Failure to pay the rent on time.
- Using the property for activities other than those previously agreed with the landlord, or for carrying out illegal, immoral or dishonest acts.
- Carrying out any building works, which have not been approved by the landlord.
- Sub-letting or lending out of the property, totally or partially, without the landlord's consent.

- Sub-letting the property for a higher rent than that which has been approved by the landlord.
- Leaving the house unoccupied for more than a year.

A landlord can also give notice for the tenant to leave when:

- The house is required for their personal use or for that of their family.
- They are intending to carry out major renovation works for which they are already in possession of a licence from the local authorities.

After having placed a copy of the rental contact with the local tax office, as detailed above, a landlord must then declare his or her rental income in their annual tax return (*IRS*).

There are a number of tax benefits and allowable expenses, which a landlord can take advantage of. A financial adviser will be able to provide advice on this, as well as a landlord's liabilities.

For more information on the law governing long-term renting you can consult the *NRAU* (*Novo Regime do Arrendamento Urbano*) government website at *www.arrendamento.gov.pt/nrau*. It is currently only available in Portuguese.

Holiday Rental

Holiday rentals are for holidaymakers or those who only wish to stay for a few weeks or months. The properties are usually furnished *(mobiliado)* and the rental agreement will normally include the utilities.

In the summer months, particularly in resort areas, these can be very difficult to come by and when they are available the prices tend to be very high. Outside the summer months you will find things a lot easier with many landlords keen to fill the empty autumn and winter months. However, should you begin renting during these off peak months, be warned that your landlord may not be keen to extend your contract into the summer period.

You will need to sign a rental agreement and if it is a long stay of more than a few weeks then you may be required to pay one month's rent in advance with another month's rent as a deposit.

Short-term rental agreements do not give a tenant the same rights as a long-term contract. If you do not speak good Portuguese, then you should get this document translated by an independent translator before agreeing to sign.

There are three categories for short-term holiday rental properties and these are:

a. Apartments – individual, or blocks of apartments.

b. Houses – standalone family homes.
c. Guest houses – rooms are individual units.

Anyone wishing to rent out one of the above types of property will need to submit a request for permission to the local council (*câmara municipal*) along with the following:

- ❑ Identification of ownership.
- ❑ A certificate from a registered technician proving that the gas and electricity installations are in compliance with Portuguese regulations.
- ❑ Property plans.
- ❑ Habitation licence (*licença de habitação*).
- ❑ The *caderneta predial* for the property.

There is also a distinction made according to accommodation capacity, i.e. those with 50 people or less and those with more than 50 people. If the capacity is more than 50 people, then there must also be a fire safety project submitted.

The request will be stamped and then you are free to rent out the property. The local council will usually carry out an inspection within 60 days of submitting the request to make sure that the property complies with certain standards and regulations.

When the council is satisfied the property meets all the requirements it will issue a plate with the initials '*AL*' (*Alojamento Local*) on, which must be displayed outside the property.

A holiday rental property must conform to the following:

- Have fire safety equipment, e.g. a fire extinguisher and fire blanket, a first aid box, instruction manuals for appliances and emergency telephone numbers.
- Be in good general condition, both inside and out, furnished to a decent standard and have good standards of cleanliness and hygiene.
- Be connected to the mains sewage system or have a septic tank *(fossa).*
- Have clean running water.
- Each unit/room must have a window to the outside for ventilation.
- Locks on the doors both for security and privacy.
- Bed linen and towels should be changed at least once a week and whenever there is a client changeover.
- A minimum of one bathroom for every three bedrooms; each containing a toilet, washbasin and bath or shower.
- Rules and regulations of the property and condominium displayed (where applicable), and general information on services provided, etc.
- Have a complaints book *(livro de reclamações).*

CASE STUDY: DAVID HINMAN

An expat with a difference: *Olá,* I'm David, I'm English, and my wife Isabel is Portuguese. We met and married in London in the late 1980s, when both in our 30s. For more than a decade we visited Portugal once or twice a year and constantly dreamed of retiring there one day. Those were fantastic holidays, and we did — for a few years in the mid 1990s — own a small holiday apartment in the Algarve, but sold it in order to invest in a bigger home in London. In 2001, I found myself out of a job and our dream of retiring to Portugal became reality.

Both in our late 40s at that time, we sold our London home, car and everything that wouldn't fit in the back of the removal van, and started a new life in Lisbon. Although Isabel has family in Lisbon — a lovely, kind and helpful sister — we found getting ourselves organised with a new home, car, GP, permits, licences and all that red tape rather more time-consuming and frustrating than we had imagined. For Isabel, being Portuguese didn't mean a lot when it came to making sense of the system as she had spent most of her adult life in London. However, I do believe the fact she is Portuguese meant we got more than our fair share of nods and winks from property developers, agents, lawyers and accountants. One must remember that Portugal has an unfortunate modern history, as for nearly half a century — up until the revolution of 1974 — its people lived under a corrupt regime.

Following the revolution, everyone wanted a share in this corrupt way of life. The EEC rescued the country in 1986, but old habits die hard.

Within about six months of moving to Portugal, we had bought two brand-new apartments in Lisbon; one to rent out and one to live in. The rental was long-term, which means under Portuguese law that the tenant has the right to stay for up to five years. This means that it's not only a potentially long-term commitment for you, the landlord, but also that you should charge a high rent from the outset as you are allowed to increase it annually by no more than the rate of inflation (officially 3% or 4% but in reality something higher).

Our first tenant moved out after nearly two years and we decided to sell that property and buy one in a new development on the Cascais coast for us to live in. After moving to Cascais, we had a tenant in our Lisbon property for another couple of years. This long-term renting was working out well for us and we were attracting foreign businessmen through letting agents with a dot.com presence.

In 2006, after nearly five years of Portuguese life and just the two long-term rental experiences, we had some serious thought about our future. Did we really want to spend the rest of our lives there? We were making enough to live quite comfortably, but saving hardly a cent. Both our properties were of the sought-after kind but were not increasing in value half as fast as London property might. Neither of us had found a proper job and I was struggling with the language. I had a blood disorder, which was having no effect on me at that time, but would have led to something serious without proper diagnosis and treatment, which is simply unavailable on the Portuguese NHS and almost certainly unavailable at any Portuguese private hospital too. Isabel is proud to be Portuguese (all Portuguese are!), loves being in Portugal and plans to spend many a future holiday on Portugal's beaches, but she confesses to favour life in England. So we sold up and moved back.

We had a wonderful five years in Portugal and have absolutely no regrets. We are now back in London as happier and spiritually healthier beings. The whole exercise didn't make sense financially as we've had to go down the London property ladder, but hey, we lived in the sun doing nothing for five years.

My advice to anyone thinking of moving to Portugal:

You must go with every intention of staying and making a success of it, but if you do return, you have not failed. If anyone's failed it was he who never tried.

Don't burn your bridges in the UK — things like keeping a bank account open will make life a whole lot simpler if you do go back, and you may consider things like paying voluntary national insurance contributions (if that is still allowed) beneficial.

The proverbial grass is no greener. It just looks, feels and tastes different.

Boa sorte!

David Hinman, London (previously Lisbon)

Residency

In the last few years Portugal has finally come in line with other EU countries and implemented the EU Directive 2004/58/EC. Therefore, immigration for EU citizens should be fairly straightforward. However, for non-EU citizens other rules will apply.

Under the new system a person no longer has to attend the immigration office (*Servico de Estrangeiros e Fronteiras – SEF*) in their area but can now go to their nearest council *(câmara municipal)* or parish council *(freguesia)* to make the *initial* residency application.

Visits

For visits of up to three months only a passport is required.

Initial Residency Certificate

After three months, and within 30 days, you can then apply for an initial residency certificate at your local council *(câmara municipal)* or parish council *(freguesia)*. According to most councils the only documentation that is required is a passport or national ID card and your Portuguese fiscal Nº, obtained from the local *Serviço das Finanças* (see the *Tax Office — Serviço das Finanças* section of the *What's What* chapter). You simply have to make a self-declaration regarding whether you are employed, self-employed or have other means to live, whether you have health insurance (if not entitled to the Portuguese health system) and other details regarding your education and family.

However, it may be best to call ahead to check with your particular local council as to which documents they need, as some also seem to request the European health card, as well as proof of address and income.

You will then be issued with an A4 paper certificate, which is valid for five years. This does not mean that you have to give up residency in your own country and is purely a registration *not* a definitive residency permit. You should carry this document with you at all times.

Permanent Residency Card

If you are still residing in Portugal after five years and wish to continue to do so, you can then apply within 30 days for a residency permit at your nearest immigration office (*Serviço de Estrangeiros e Fronteiras – SEF*). The documents required are a passport or national ID card, two passport type photos and your previous residency certificate. However, you may also be asked for your last tax (*IRS*) return and other documents, so it may be best to call ahead first to double check with the *SEF* in your area.

You will then be issued with a card *(cartão de residência)*. This is renewed after 10 years, but is merely a formality to update your photo and refresh the document.

Once you have a permanent residency card, you should inform the *SEF*, as well as the local tax office, if you permanently leave Portugal.

Immigration Office – Serviço de Estrangeiros e Fronteiras (SEF)

The immigration office (*Serviços de Estrangeiros e Fronteiras – SEF*) have a website at *www.sef.pt*.

You can use this site not only for up to date residency and immigration information, but also to make an appointment online to renew your residency at the nearest *SEF*. Click on the British flag in the top left-hand corner and then on *Online appointment in a SEF Delegation* in the box on the right-hand side of the page.

Alternatively, you can telephone the *SEF* on 808 202 653 from a landline or 808 962 690 from a mobile. You can then select option one for an appointment or option two for further information. The service is available in various languages, including English, French, Russian, Ukrainian and Romanian.

Some *SEF's* are also now able to take your photos, but make sure that you check before you go that your nearest office has this facility available. If not, you will still have to take along your own photos as before.

Non-EU Citizens

For non-EU citizens you should consult your particular embassy or Portuguese consulate in your home country for details of your entry and visa requirements, as these can differ from country to country.

To gain entry to Portugal you will need at least a passport (valid for more than three months after the intended period of stay), an entry visa and proof of means of subsistence.

There are several different types of visa, such as short stay, transit, residence, study and work. If you intend to live in Portugal, then it is advisable to obtain a residence visa.

Once you have an entry visa you can then consult the nearest *SEF* for further immigration information and requirements, which will often include (amongst other things) a criminal background check.

An electronic residency card has now been introduced for non-EU citizens, which is similar to the Portuguese citizens' new, all-in-one, 'super' ID card. It has a chip that not only stores residency information, but also fiscal and social security details. Renewals of this card can be dealt with as per the information supplied above for EU citizens, i.e. the online appointment system or by telephone.

Documents required for this card include a valid passport, fiscal Nº, proof of address and income and two passport type photos. However, as previously mentioned, it is always best to check with the office that you will be attending as to the documents required, in order to not have the wasted trip.

Tax Implications

It is beyond the scope of this book to go into great detail about personal taxation, but it should nevertheless be noted that there is a difference between a residency certificate/card and fiscal residency.

You become a tax resident only if you stay more than 183 days a year in Portugal, either continuously or interrupted, or if you stay less than 183 days, but have a permanent place of residence established by the year end.

Whereas permanent, fiscal residents are taxed on their worldwide income, non-residents will only pay tax on their earned income inside Portugal. This will usually be at a 25% flat tax rate. Portugal has signed treaties with many countries in order to avoid double taxation, so you should receive a tax credit in your home country to avoid paying twice. You must declare your income in the country where it is generated.

You can also obtain a certificate of fiscal residency online in order to prove your tax residency in Portugal to other countries to avoid double taxation. Go to the *Portal das Finanças website* at *www.portaldasfinancas.gov.pt*. Once you have signed in, click on *Serviços* on the left-hand side and then *Obter* and *Certidões,* followed by *Consultar Certidões*.

In the *Certidão* box click on the arrow and highlight *Residência Fiscal,* and then enter the date of the request (*Data do Pedido*). Finally, click on *Continuar* at the bottom. See the *Tax Office – Serviço das Finanças* section of the *What's What* chapter to find out about how to create an account.

If you are a tax resident in two countries at the same time then this will be resolved under the international tax treaties' rules.

Taxation is a very complex and personal subject and so it is advisable to obtain tax advice before relocating to Portugal. This advice should preferably be from someone knowledgeable in both Portuguese taxation and the taxation system in your current country of residence.

You should advise the tax authorities upon leaving your home country permanently – you may even be due for a refund.

On arriving in Portugal and starting work, or a business, you should inform the tax office *(serviço das finanças)* as soon as possible. Portugal has a PAYE system of income tax, whereby an employee's tax is held at source and the self-employed must adhere to a personal system of declaration.

Tax (*IRS*) declarations can be made by paper or online at the *Portal das Finanças* website, once you have signed in. The return is known as a *Modelo 3*. There are different dates for submission depending on whether it is done online or paper and according to the type of income. Check either the *Portal das Finanças* website for the date, or with a professional financial adviser or accountant.

Traditionally a tax evader's paradise, Portugal is now beginning to get to grips with those who try to avoid paying – particularly foreigners. So be warned! Seek good advice rather than risk getting caught. You will not only have to pay back the tax owed, but may also suffer heavy fines, or worse get permanently 'black-listed'.

CASE STUDY: BEN TAYLOR

My wife, Louise, and I spent several years planning our move to Portugal. We are perhaps not your typical migrants to the country, both being in our early thirties.

We were doing perfectly well in London. My wife had a well-paid job and I had built up a successful, though maddeningly stressful, IT business. We lived in a good area of London, drove a nice, shiny car and had money in the bank.

Due to my overwhelming need to constantly chase the sunshine, we took plenty of short holidays, usually to Portugal (once we discovered the country we didn't really want to go anywhere else). Sadly, these breaks were invariably interrupted by calls from frantic clients and the constant vibrating of my Blackberry.

One day, we were on holiday on the beautiful Portuguese island of Porto Santo, off the coast of Madeira. It was about 5pm, and as I sat on my lounger I looked out to the sea and saw a local man sitting on the edge of the shore with his young son. They looked so content.

At that moment I had a terrifying vision of the future! Our lives in London were on a common path, and I knew exactly what was five years further down it: a bigger house in a slightly more affluent area of London, a bigger, shinier car and a bit more money in the bank. Alongside these things would be longer hours, a Blackberry that vibrated ever more frequently and, worst of all, children who would have closer relationships with their childminders than with us.

I had seen so many lives like this and I didn't want any part of it. I wanted to be that Portuguese man sitting on the shore with his son.

We spent the next three years planning and researching. My wife was very fortunate to have a progressive employer who accepted that she could perform her role from a distance, making full use of technologies such as Skype. That was the first *major* hurdle jumped – it is difficult to find well-paid employment in Portugal, even with fluent Portuguese.

I put a plan in place to trim down my business and diversify into web-based work that I, too, could do from a distance – all with the emphasis on not taking my stressful life to Portugal with me!

After these years of getting everything in order, building up an emergency fund, and frantically 'ebaying' and 'carbooting' our vast amount of clutter, the day finally arrived for our move. We bid sad farewells to our friends, some of whom I suspect thought we were crazy to turn our backs on London.

We decided to rent initially, with the intention of trying both the Algarve and the Silver Coast before buying a property. This turned out to be a good plan, although not for the reasons we expected. The traditional townhouse we moved into first ended up being a damp, mouldy disaster when the first few months of our sunny, Portuguese dream turned out to be the wettest Algarve winter since 1870!

After four months of water leaking under doors and windows every time it rained, and new mould patches appearing daily, it was time to move on! We now live in a modern apartment in Conceição de Tavira, exactly the kind of place we were adamant we didn't want to live in before we moved. We adore it. Renting has allowed us to experiment a bit, and I would strongly recommend it to anyone planning a permanent move. Our village is small, but most things we need are only a 15-minute cycle away, including a beautiful beach accessed by a 60-second boat ride with a friendly local fisherman.

How have we found the experience so far? In the main it has lived up to our expectations, but I would say it has been marginally more stressful than we had expected. Everyone tells you the bureaucracy is a nightmare — it truly is. When we visit government buildings we now treat every tiny bit of progress we make as a step forward; expecting anything to happen quickly in Portugal is the path to disappointment!

What are the plus points? Going for a cooling swim at lunchtime, having barbecues several times a week and experiencing a different beautiful beach every weekend. We dreamed about all of these things during the three years of planning — and they have all come true! In particular we have fallen in love with Portuguese food and with the plentiful markets selling fresh, local produce, which tastes so much better than anything you can buy in an English supermarket.

What advice would we give people planning to move here? Most importantly, do as much as you can to learn Portuguese – every extra word makes your life easier. Secondly, try to slow down your pace – don't expect anything to happen quickly, and realise that while doubts do come creeping up on you in the early days, they will diminish. Most importantly, eat some sardines, drink that delicious, cheap wine, and enjoy the sunshine!

Ben Taylor, Conceição de Tavira, Algarve

www.movingtoportugal.org

www.foodandwineportugal.com

About Gabrielle

I was born in London and attended Nonsuch High School for Girls in Cheam. Being a rather free-spirited person and finding the constraints and curriculum of an all girls grammar school a bit too much for me, I left at 16 to start a job in structural engineering in London.

However, I later returned to academic life and obtained both a BA (Hons) in Sports Studies and History and an MSc in Sports Science. During this time I also became a top class runner, gaining an Athletics National Championship (AAA) medal in the 3000m and various vests for road and track. As well as pursuing my athletics, I spent time as a part-time teacher and coach, and worked in a specialist running shop in Brighton.

Unfortunately, I had to retire from athletics due to an Achilles tendon injury and with my running career behind me I decided to do some travelling.

I have been lucky enough to spend time in: France, Belgium, Italy, Spain, the Canary Islands, the Balearic Islands, Portugal, Greece and the Greek Islands. I have also visited Central America.

I learnt French and Spanish at school, and Italian and Portuguese during my travels. I don't speak any fluently, but I love dabbling in languages as I think it tells you so much about a nation, as well as being a great way to integrate.

My parents moved to Portugal in 2000 and so I found myself spending more and more time there. I began to get involved with various things, especially in relation to bureaucracy and property purchase problems. It therefore seemed the logical next step to write a book, in order to pass on the knowledge that I had gained in this area.

This is my second edition and I have tried to make it even more informative than the first. Not an easy task when things change so often in Portugal and when there are different local interpretations of regulations.

I am now based in North London and believe my travels have made me appreciate my native land more – warts and all! However, I fully understand why people want to try living somewhere else and it is definitely something I'd encourage people to do.

I am currently writing some other titles and spend my free time drinking wine with friends, going to the gym, swimming and going to rock and metal gigs.

Appendices

IMT (Purchase Tax) 2011

The tables below show the different scales of purchase tax (*imposto municipal sobre transmissões onerosas de imóveis — IMT*) for urban property as of 2011. Non-permanent occupation refers to holiday homes and second homes as opposed to permanent occupation, which refers to your primary place of residence.

Permanent Occupation	**Rate**	**Deduction**
Up to €92,407	0%	€0
€92,407 – €126,403	2%	€1,848.14
€126,403 – €172,348	5%	€5,640.23
€172,348 – €287,213	7%	€9,087.19
€287,213 – €574,323	8%	€11,959.32
> €574,323	6%	€0
Non Permanent Occupation	**Rate**	**Deduction**
Up to €92,407	1%	€0
€92,407 – €126,403€	2%	€924.07
€126,403 – €172,348	5%	€4,716.16
€172,348 – €287,213	7%	€8,163.12
€287,213 – €550,836	8%	€11,035.25
> €550,836	6%	€0

Note the following rates apply for other types of property:

a. A building plot or land to build an urban property is at a 6.5% flat rate.

b. A rustic property and agricultural land is at a 5.0% flat rate.

c. An offshore property in a white-listed jurisdiction is at an 8% flat rate and a black-listed one at a 15% flat rate.

Property Purchase Checklist

(Make A Copy For Each Property You View.
Remember To Take Photos, Video & GPS Coordinates)

This property purchase checklist should be used in conjunction with your legal representative's checks.

Notes

Property

- Price
- Bedrooms
- Bathrooms
- Total Nº Of Rooms
- Covered Area (m2)
- Uncovered Area (logradouro/ envelope & land m2)
- Electricity
- Water
  - a) Mains
  - b) Borehole
  - c) Well
  - d) Cisterna/Water Tank
    - i. Neighbours Supply
    - ii. Bombeiros Supply
- Phone
- Internet
- Gas
- Mains Drainage
- Septic Tank
- Swimming Pool
- Garage

Notes

Location
- Countryside
- Village
- Coast
- Town/City

Access
- Poor
- Fair
- Good

Transport
- Roads/Motorways
- Trains
- Buses
- Airport

Amenities
- Medical
    - a) Hospital
    - b) Health Centre/Drs.
- Schools/Colleges
- Entertainment
- Restaurants/Cafés

Reason
- Investment
- Rental
- Holidays
- For Family
- To Live

Notes

Type

- Plot To Build
- Ruin To Renovate
- New Build
- Off Plan
- Resale

Type of Land

- Urban
- Rustic
- Agricultural
- Ecological
- Mixed %s

In Working Order

- Boiler
- Heating System
- Water Heating System
- Electrics
- Fitted Appliances
- Borehole Pump
- Cisterna/Water Tank
- Well
- Water Quality
- Septic Tank
- Phone Line
- Internet
- Swimming Pool Equipment
- Irrigation System

Notes

Further Checks

- Rights Of Way
- Adjoining Neighbours Been Asked
- Boundaries Clearly Marked
- Property Map Checked
- Survey Of Boundaries Required
- Survey Of Property Required
- View Likely To Remain
- PDM Checked
- Building/Planning Permission Obtained For All Works Planned
- Builder's Warranty
- Building(s) All Legal
- Swimming Pool Legal
- Borehole Legal
- Condominium Charges Up To Date
- Condominium Rules & Regulations
- All Utility Bills & IMI (council tax) Up To Date

Current Document Checks

- Certidão de Teor/Registo Predial
- Caderneta(s)
- Property Map
- Current Escritura
- Habitation Licence or Pre-1951 Certificate
- Ficha Técnica de Habitação
- Swimming Pool Construction & Utilization Licences

Notes

- Borehole Licence
- Borehole & Septic Tank Registered
- Energy Efficiency Certificate

Check Credentials

- Real Estate Agent's AMI Nº
- UK Company's Registered Nº
- Private Vendor
- Builder's Alvará Nº & Company Nº
- Lawyer or Solicitador's Cédula Nº

Purchase Budget Calculator

(Make A Copy & Fill It In)

Property Price ______________________________

IMT Purchase Tax (see 2011 IMT table) ___________

IVA (VAT 21% for new properties only) __________

Legal Fees (1 to 2.5 % of property value) __________

Notary Fees* ________________________________

Deed Registration Fees* _______________________

Stamp Duty (0.8%) ____________________________

Survey If Carried Out (approx. €500) ______________

* Together approx. 1 to 2% of property value

Remember that you will also have to budget for IMI (council tax), and condominium and mortgage fees (where applicable), as well as your everyday maintenance and running costs.

Lightning Source UK Ltd.
Milton Keynes UK
UKOW031921190712

196282UK00010B/7/P